Faith
in the
Making

The Bible Reading Fellowship
15 The Chambers, Vineyard
Abingdon OX14 3FE
brf.org.uk

The Bible Reading Fellowship (BRF) is a Registered Charity (233280)

ISBN 978 0 85746 555 9
First published 2018
10 9 8 7 6 5 4 3 2 1 0
All rights reserved

Acknowledgements
Unless otherwise stated, scripture quotations are taken from The Holy Bible, New
International Version (Anglicised edition) copyright © 1979, 1984, 2011 by Biblica.
Used by permission of Hodder & Stoughton Publishers, an Hachette UK company.
All rights reserved. 'NIV' is a registered trademark of Biblica. UK trademark number
1448790.

Scripture quotations taken from the Amplified® Bible (AMP), Copyright © 2015 by
The Lockman Foundation. Used by permission. www.Lockman.org.

Scripture quotations taken from *THE MESSAGE*, copyright © 1993, 1994, 1995, 1996,
2000, 2001, 2002 by Eugene H. Peterson. Used by permission of NavPress. All rights
reserved. Represented by Tyndale House Publishers, Inc.

Scripture taken from the New King James Version®. Copyright © 1982 by Thomas
Nelson. Used by permission. All rights reserved.

Scripture taken from The Voice™. Copyright © 2008 by Ecclesia Bible Society. Used by
permission. All rights reserved.

Every effort has been made to trace and contact copyright owners for material used
in this resource. We apologise for any inadvertent omissions or errors, and would
ask those concerned to contact us so that full acknowledgement can be made in
the future.

A catalogue record for this book is available from the British Library

Printed and bound by CPI Group (UK) Ltd, Croydon CR0 4YY

Faith in the Making

Praying it, talking it and living it

Lyndall Bywater

Foreword by Danielle Strickland

Contents

Foreword

I'm about twelve years old and a few of my friends are huddled around the turntable in my bedroom listening to the greatest-hits record and belting out the lyrics of our favourite song, 'Holding Out for a Hero'. We join with full gusto the dynamic voice of Bonnie Tyler, singing together at the top of our lungs with joy and abandon.

It felt innocent enough at the time, but I'm afraid that song might have been more dangerous than it appeared. I learned, like so many of us, that there is someone *else* who is stronger, better and more capable to do what should be done. A hero. This root belief, taught through our culture, turns us all into helpless spectators of our own lives. The idea that there is someone else better, faster and stronger coming to help almost always leaves us watching terrible things happen to people in this weary world instead of pitching in to help.

What are we doing while young children are bought and sold like cattle on the fastest-growing crime circuit called human trafficking? We are waiting for a hero.

What are we doing about extreme poverty that leaves hundreds of thousands of people dead in its ugly, evil wake? We are holding out for a hero.

What are we doing about the millions of people trapped in fatalism and religious systems leading them to accept their god-ordained fates of exploitation and poverty? We are, as I belted out with my young girlfriends, holding out for a hero.

Even more sinister than making us passive in the face of the injustices that threaten our globe, this idea of heroism can make us feel like we have no part to play in the world. We feel small and insignificant in the face of danger or obstacles. When we encounter pain or difficulties we sit it out, because there must be someone else coming. Many of our own destinies are dormant, because we are still holding out for a type of hero that has to be strong and has to be tough and has to be someone other than us.

This is why I love this book, not to mention the woman who wrote it. God introduces us to heroes of the faith – men and women that we like to put on pedestals and cast as amazing people who were stronger and more able than us. When we think of them that way we miss the whole point about why God chose them. But when we take a closer look, which is what this book invites you to do, it helps us understand something that will change everything. These heroes of biblical proportions, they were normal people. Living in their own time and place in history, they were the average Joes. They really were. You can tell by the way they got it wrong so many times, and complained and were confused and doubted and feared and were cowardly at key moments – cringeworthy cowardice at really important moments.

And it wasn't a mistake. God wasn't surprised that the hero he had chosen ended up being, well, simply human. The reason God tells the whole truth when he had these stories written is that God's word about heroes is so different from any other word we've heard about heroes before; so different from the superhero brand of 'salvation' that ranges from stage crusaders to type-A business leaders, megachurch pastors with super-shiny teeth and non-profit leaders with capes, saving the world. In other words, we've learned that heroes are people who aren't like the rest of us.

What we have believed about heroes is wrong. Simply fantasy. Heroes are real people who do real things in real life that change things. I believe in heroes. The woman who wrote this book is one of mine. What's coming in the following pages is an exploration of living a heroic life in real time. We have never needed heroes more than right now. The world is desperate for people who will give what they have and who they are for the benefit of others. What is most remarkable about this book is that it's an exploration that leads to an invitation. It's simple really. I'm not holding out for a hero anymore. I get it now. A hero is not someone coming to rescue me. A hero is someone who responds to God's invitation to use what they have and who they are to help someone else.

For everyone reading this book, of course, that's you. You are the hero. You are the one the whole world, and definitely your neighbour, your child or your community, is holding out for. You don't have to be strong or smart, because the invitation comes from the only true and perfect hero, who is smarter and stronger and wiser and bigger than any of us could even imagine.

God is recruiting a team of heroes to brave the ordinary elements of our lives to live for something greater than ourselves. And that is heroic. You'll discover in this book the recipe of living a life beyond the status quo. These words will awaken a deep hunger already inside you to live the life you've always dreamed was possible if you were stronger and faster and younger. Whatever you've been waiting for, most likely the cause of the hesitancy is rooted somewhere in the notion that the hero you seek is outside of you – when, as Lyndall herself discovered, it has been inside you the whole time.

I'm so happy I stopped spectating and joined the heroic team of ordinary radicals changing the world by defying the status quo and spreading goodness with our everyday lives. What Lyndall offers us is not just well-written words, although this book is beautifully written. She offers us a life example of someone ordinary and spectacular at the same time. Her life is a powerful invitation to a preposterous plan of holy mischief that will impact the world with God's goodness through your life.

If ever I go bungee jumping again, I'm taking Lyndall with me. But if that can't happen, this book will be my reminder of the leap of faith we are currently taking together. I hope you'll join us.

Danielle Strickland

Introduction

'Just keep stepping backwards,' he said. 'You'll be fine.'

I said various unkind things in my head, and took a tiny, terrified step backwards.

'That's it! Just a couple more steps like that and you'll be on your way.'

The 'he' in question was my abseiling instructor, and the 'on your way' in question was the descent of a 50-foot cliff. Suffice it to say, many more minutes and many more dark thoughts passed before I finally made it over the edge.

It might surprise you to know, then, that that abseiling adventure was one of the most amazing experiences of my life. Once I had conquered the tricky bit, where you go from being vertical at the top to being horizontal on the way down, I thoroughly enjoyed the sensation of dangling in mid-air, with nothing but a rope at my belt, a sheer cliff face at my feet and a patient instructor at my side.

Scroll forward a year or so and you will find a 14-year-old me standing in the warm, shallow waters of a Greek beach, being strapped into a harness which will, in due course, be attached to a parachute and tethered to the back of a speedboat. That speedboat is about to make its way around the bay, with me streaming out behind it, somewhere up in the sky. At this point, you might conclude that either I had rather cruel parents or I had always harboured a secret longing to fly. I am happy to say it was the latter. Whether dangling from a rope against a cliff face, parascending over the Aegean Sea or being hurled through the air by a particularly ambitious rollercoaster,

I have always loved the sensation of defying gravity. I should perhaps mention at this point that I am blind, and my friends and family often tell me that this might just be a contributing factor in my ability to stand terrifying heights and gut-rearranging drops. They're probably right. Be it my blindness or just the wiring in my brain, I have always loved finding myself in places it shouldn't be possible to be.

In contrast to the abseiling and parascending, I remember finding Christianity a rather pedestrian business when I was a child. My family have always gone to church, and I loved it. I never had one of those teenaged rebellions where you flatly refuse to get out of bed on a Sunday morning, and I never doubted that Christianity was true. I chose to follow Jesus from my earliest days in Sunday school, and I have never once regretted or reneged on that choice. I loved the values, I learned the rules and I lived out the practices to the best of my ability. It was wholesome, but if I'm honest it was also boring, most of the time. The Christians around me were pragmatic, down-to-earth people who loved Jesus and lived faithful lives, but something in me railed against this grounded approach to faith. After all, I wanted to be able to fly.

The take off, when it eventually came, happened at university. I had joined an interdenominational student group, and our leaders suggested that we study the 'heroes of faith' in Hebrews 11. I began the term convinced that this would be another of those worthy self-improvement programmes, where you are gently shamed into shape by a carefully selected parade of superheroes who've all made an excellent job of doing life with God. Instead, I finished the term having met with a bunch of completely normal people who soared their way to impossible things because they lost sight of their own limitations and got caught up in the bigness of God.

The stories in Hebrews 11 seemed to point to a kind of Christianity which was less about rules and values and more about possibilities for changing the world. While I'd always understood that being a Christian would mean I could do good to those around me – maybe even tell them about Jesus one day – I had never understood that it could mean the things of God's kingdom starting to happen in the place where I lived. The idea consumed me, and it has never left me. The code and the values still matter to me, but what gets me out of bed in the morning is the passionate belief that there is so much more to this life than I have yet seen – so much more of God's kingdom to come, not just at the end of time but right now.

US president Abraham Lincoln and his wife Mary had a long-held ambition to visit Scotland. Some years after her husband's assassination, Mary finally got to do the tour she'd always wanted to do. When she'd completed it, she said, 'Beautiful, glorious Scotland has spoilt me for every other country.' That was my experience of reading Hebrews 11. It felt like a tour around a country I'd always wanted to visit, and when I'd finally done it, I was spoilt for anything less. The life I had been living, and the limits I had been living within, suddenly didn't feel like life any more. As I dug deep into those stories of the heroes, during that year at university, I became hungry for something more than just living well for Jesus. I started to want to see what might be possible if I let God take me beyond myself.

And then, somewhere in the middle of our 'heroes' series, a man called Thomas Hamilton walked into a primary school in Dunblane, in 'beautiful, glorious Scotland', and shot dead 16 pupils and a teacher. It was one of the worst mass murders in Britain's history, and it shook me to the core. How could any world be broken enough for that kind of thing to happen? How could any man be broken enough to choose to slaughter children?

As I wrestled with the questions, I suddenly found Hebrews 11 had taken on a whole new meaning for me. If this was the kind of world where someone could wander into a school at 9.35 am on a Wednesday morning, massacre 17 people, injure 15 more and then kill himself, it was a world that needed some serious heroes. I watched people on the news trying to make sense of it all, and I prayed as best I could for those families who had had their little ones torn away from them. Bit by bit I understood that this shattered world of ours needs people who can see beyond the shards of despair and defeat to a different reality. It needs people who have the compassion to sit with those in pain, and the courage to stand up and lead the way to a place where hope puts us all back together again.

There's a reason why children love to read fantasy fiction. It's because it speaks of the possibility of other exciting worlds right alongside us in our everyday lives. Whether it's C.S. Lewis' Narnia, a magical kingdom just the other side of a wardrobe, or Philippa Pearce's midnight garden, where Tom finds a whole other time and place full of fun and beauty, or J.K. Rowling's Harry Potter series, where children suddenly find they have a role in overthrowing evil and changing their world for the better, authors have long known that children have a natural affinity for the idea that this reality isn't all there is. Children have no problem believing in other worlds and other realities, living easily with one foot in a different dimension.

Somehow we tend to lose that art as we get to grips with adulthood. We assume all those fantasy worlds were childish nonsense and we settle down to accepting that the sum total of reality is what we can see and understand. Yet it's that obsession with other realities which the writer to the Hebrews commends, over and over again. Most of the heroes mentioned could have been accused of being at best naive and at worst delusional because of the seemingly impossible realities they believed in: Noah lived in a desert but believed in a flood; Abraham and Sarah had no children of their own, yet they believed that their descendants would spread out all over the world; Moses' people had been subjugated in slavery for 400 years, yet he believed they could be set free and sent home to their promised land. With the value of hindsight, it all looks pretty doable to us, but in their day these men and women could have been accused of living in a fantasy world.

And that's what the writer to the Hebrews calls living 'by faith'.

Faith means so many different things to so many different people. Faith is the thread which runs through all those hero stories, and it's the thread which the writer to the Hebrews invites us to grab hold of and weave into our own lives. Yet, for many of us, it's a word we shy away from. If you're anything like me, then faith falls into the same category as words like 'diet' and 'savings' – words that simultaneously inspire me and make me feel slightly guilty. Then again, you may be someone for whom the very word 'faith' triggers fear and a sense of failure, because it has been used too often as a stick to beat you with. If you were ever told that you weren't healed because you lacked faith, or that you went into debt because you didn't believe hard enough, then the very concept of 'faith' may be terrifying. Before we go any further then, we should establish some basics about faith.

The first verse of Hebrews 11 gives a definition of faith which launches us straight up into the wide open blue sky of limitless possibility:

> Now faith is confidence in what we hope for and assurance about what we do not see.
> HEBREWS 11:1

According to this definition, faith has something of the 'beyond' about it. You've probably heard it said that faith isn't faith if you're believing in something you already know to be possible. If you're aiming for something doable, something you can see and reach in your own strength, then what you're employing is skill, strategy, strength and even courage, but not faith. Faith only comes into play when we leap off the end of what we know to be achievable. It was in those packed meetings in that overheated church hall every Sunday night that I realised I had been longing to go beyond – beyond the sensible, doable Christianity I'd been living – to a place of risk and absolute reliance on God. And it was sitting in front of my TV in my cluttered university bedroom, crying my eyes out over the Dunblane massacre, that I realised I needed to go beyond my comfortable, bless-me-now Christianity, to a place where my faith might actually help other people find new realities. I didn't want to know what the world would be like if I practised a doable kind of Christianity; I wanted to know what the world would be like if I jumped off the end of my own greatest efforts and catapulted myself into gravity-defying dreams of the impossible.

And it was as I started living that way that I learned the other crucial ingredient of faith. It has something of the 'beyond' about it, but it also has something of the 'beside' about it.

If you've ever stepped out in faith, you won't need me to tell you that it can be an unpredictable business. Sometimes it goes the way we want, and we find ourselves face-to-face with the thing we'd hoped for. But sometimes the wind of God's purposes blows us on to a whole new course, setting us down in a landscape which we haven't foreseen, and which, if we're honest, we don't want to see. To go beyond our own limits is to fly by God's instruments, not our own.

Looking back now, I can see countless snapshots of myself over the years, baffled by faith leaps which left me staggering instead of soaring. Yet as I scan those memories, I can also remember the intense feeling of God's nearness: pacing the university campus, putting off doing something I was dreading; lying in a hospital bed after a traumatic accident; grieving so many friends who died, despite our faith-filled prayers; waiting for the miracle which never came – each situation so painful and bewildering, yet each one crackling with the sense of God's nearness. In this I am blessed. Many people rarely sense the closeness of God, either in their best or worst times. For me it has been the comforting reminder that we are never asked to take our faith leaps alone. There is one who leaps with us, and who remains by our side, whether we soar, bounce or crash-land.

Faith comes from God, and it has two hallmarks: it holds tight to hope and it draws near to a friend. The Hebrews 11 heroes were all hoping for something. Faith is holding tight to what we hope for. No matter how many times the world says, 'This is reality and this is all there is', faith says: 'I'm holding tight to my belief that there is more to come.' When so-called reality says despair is the end of the story, faith says that there can be light and hope again. When so-called reality says that things can't be changed, faith says that things can be made new. Living by faith means holding on to that better, brighter, hope-filled reality and shaping your life around it.

But the Hebrews 11 heroes also had a friendship. The God who sparks faith in us isn't some talisman or good-luck charm; he is a friend. He doesn't want to give us superpowers; he wants to keep us company. Yes, we may well see miracles and wonders along the way, but what he most wants is for us to draw near. He wants us to stop keeping him at arm's length, and let him sweep us up in an embrace of love. After all, when you really know you're loved, a whole heap of things become possible that just weren't possible before.

The 'beyond' and the 'beside', the hope and the friendship, go together. Big hopes and dreams are wonderful things to have, and some of the most inspiring characters in history have been people who achieved things which seemed impossible, but a hope without a friend is exhausting and ultimately futile. William Wilberforce had a dream to see slavery made illegal in England, and though most people thought it impossible, he achieved a miraculous victory. Yet this courageous human-rights activist knew that he needed to draw near to God in friendship just as much as he needed to pursue his impossible dream. As he wrote in *Real Christianity*:

> It makes no sense to take the name of Christian and not cling to Christ. Jesus is not some magic charm to wear like a piece of jewelry we think will give us good luck. He is the Lord. His name is to be written on our hearts in such a powerful way that it creates within us a profound experience of His peace and a heart that is filled with His praise.

Abraham dreamed of settling his people in a new land; Moses dreamed of leading his enslaved people to freedom. Big hopes, indeed. Yet these men weren't known as 'God's heroic hopers' or 'God's impossible dreamers'; they were both known by the name 'friend of God'. It was the friendship which gave them the strength to pursue the dreams.

If hope without friendship exhausts us, then friendship without something to hope for causes us to stagnate. The Hebrews 11 heroes all caught the hope bug. They could all have stayed put and made do, but none of them did. They all set out to make a difference. Would God have loved them any less if they hadn't? Of course not. But I'm not sure it's possible to draw near to God in friendship without being infected with hope – hope for ourselves, but also hope for a world where things need putting right. To know the reality of this broken world and at the same time to know friendship with the God of hope: that's a combination which puts us in serious danger of becoming dreamers.

My third guide dog was a black Labrador called Croft, and he was somewhat prone to crises of confidence. When he was at the top of his game he was perhaps the most capable dog I ever had, but when he got an attack of the wobbles we'd have to stop and have a little reassuring chat. The truth is, he needed two things above everything else: he needed to be enthusiastic about the task in hand, and he needed to know I was there, cheering him on. As we made our way through the world together, I would often reflect on how similar we were. After all, those are the things I need too. I need enthusiasm, hope and vision; I need to know I'm living for something bigger and more significant than just getting by. And I need to know that God, the friend of my soul, is at my side, believing in me, walking with me and spurring me on. That pincer movement of hope and friendship will get me anywhere.

Throughout the course of this book, we will meet some of the characters from Hebrews 11. We will examine their hopes and dreams, and we will take a peek into their friendships with God. At the end of each section, you will find a number of suggestions for ways in which you can pray, talk and live out the things you've read about. It is my prayer, as you read, that you too will get swept up in that divine pincer movement of hoping and loving, dreaming and trusting, and that you will discover your own unique brand of heroic faith.

1

Abel and Enoch

By faith Abel brought God a better offering than Cain did. By faith he was commended as righteous, when God spoke well of his offerings. And by faith Abel still speaks, even though he is dead. By faith Enoch was taken from this life, so that he did not experience death: 'He could not be found, because God had taken him away.' For before he was taken, he was commended as one who pleased God.

HEBREWS 11:4–5

Faith ignited
Genesis 4:1–8

But Abel also brought an offering – fat portions from some of the firstborn of his flock. The Lord looked with favour on Abel and his offering...

GENESIS 4:4

I once fainted in a Mormon lady's doorway. She opened her front door, I started introducing myself, and the next thing I knew I was lying flat out in her hallway.

It happened during my university years, in those heady days when I was discovering a more 'on fire' kind of Christianity. I was a modern languages student, so had to spend a year abroad as part of my degree course, and the various universities available in France and

Switzerland had all said they thought it would be too complicated to host a blind student. Not daunted, I suggested to my bewildered tutors that I could spend a year church-planting with Operation Mobilisation in France, and to my surprise they said yes.

In those days, our favoured evangelism strategy was to go door to door selling Bibles, and that's how I ended up on the Mormon lady's doorstep. If faith is going beyond yourself and leaping into the impossible, then I was there! The Bible-selling and the conversations with total strangers were taking me so far out of my comfort zone that I was convinced some kind of exciting miracle must be just around the corner. Yet I learned another important lesson about faith that day, as I picked myself up and dusted myself down.

The lady was, of course, rather concerned about me, and insisted on inviting us in so she could give me a glass of water. All I wanted to do was go home. I was queasy, shaken and very embarrassed. But I knew a drink would probably be a good idea, so my friend and I took a seat at her kitchen table and spent half an hour chatting with her about life and Jesus, and before we left we prayed together.

I'd like to tell you that the chat and the prayer made it all worth it, and that I left feeling at peace, but that would be a lie. I cringed with embarrassment for days afterwards, and I had several furious conversations with God about just how much I disapproved of him letting me pass out in such awkward circumstances. He knew that would be one of my worst nightmares, and he could have prevented it. If he'd wanted us to sit at that lady's table and talk, he could have done it a million other ways. Why use me? Why make me so vulnerable? Why humiliate me?

I learned that day that if you ask God to make you an 'on fire' kind of Christian, he is very likely to use as his kindling something that is very dear to you; in my case, my pride.

In the introduction to Hebrews 11, before the writer gets going on those mini-biographies of the heroes, we get a glimpse of two people from the earliest days of Bible history. Abel and Enoch only get a few words each, but they seem to represent something foundational in this emerging architecture of faith, so we do well to notice them.

Cain and Abel are the first siblings mentioned in scripture, and they wasted no time getting the age-old tradition of sibling rivalry underway. Sadly, their rivalry had a dark and tragic ending. At a given moment in time, both brothers presented a sacrifice to God, each bringing something which represented the fruits of his labours: Cain some of his ripened produce, and Abel the fat from some of his newborn animals. We are told that God looked favourably on Abel and his offering, but not on Cain and his.

Much has been written about why only Abel's act of worship was acceptable to God, but the simplest explanation seems to be that it cost him something dear. Cain brought a respectable selection of good things, whereas Abel slaughtered several animals, cutting off any future value such precious assets might produce. Cain brought an offering, whereas Abel made a sacrifice.

Right at the start of this procession of heroes, we're face-to-face with a man who let his relationship with God cost him dearly. In a few verses, we'll be meeting with the dreamers – the people who were looking a long way beyond themselves and their current circumstances. We have no way of knowing whether Abel had that kind of vision. All we know is that he was a man who was prepared to lay down something precious for God. And if you know anything of shepherds or stockmen, you'll know those younglings would have been very precious to him indeed, not just as an economic asset but as something he loved and cared for.

Long before the hopes and dreams take shape, God asks us the simple question: 'Am I more important to you than the things you hold most dear?' Sometimes going 'beyond ourselves' in faith is all about big, world-changing adventures, and then sometimes it's about the equally risky and impossible business of entrusting the most precious and vulnerable parts of our lives to God.

There has also been much speculation about how God signalled his approval of Abel's sacrifice. Did he use the weather or draw huge scorecards in the sky? For the time being, we'll have to settle for guesswork, and the best guess is that he used fire, since that is how he revealed himself on so many other occasions (in the burning bush, on Mount Carmel and in the upper room at Pentecost, to name but a few). As we set out on our journey to explore the workings of faith, I am halted in wonder at that image of the divine fire of God's presence consuming the painful, precious sacrifice of a humble cattle herder. Murdered by his jealous brother, Abel didn't get to live much beyond that day, but his story is still remembered and retold, thousands of years later, perhaps because it carries the most basic ingredients of that mystery we call 'faith'.

Twenty-three years after my brush with the Mormon lady's carpet, it still serves as a reminder and a challenge. The shame has finally worn off, but the tendency to try to preserve my pride at all costs is taking a little longer to eradicate. Yet, looking back, I have to admit that those agonising moments of surrender, of sacrificing my need to look good, have also been moments when the presence of God has set fire to me in a new way. Yes, it's been uncomfortable – even painful – but it has been worth it.

At this stage, it would be tempting to dig out a nice story of how letting God singe away my pride has made the world a better place, but I will resist the temptation. You see, Abel's story isn't remembered because his sacrifice had fabulously far-reaching consequences. It is remembered because he honoured God with the best he had, and that is where it all begins.

Praying it

Surrender isn't accomplished in one easy prayer time, or even one difficult prayer time. Surrender is something we keep coming back to; it's a habit and a life rhythm. This exercise is a practical way to remind yourself of Abel's truth: that God's presence burns brightest in us when we surrender the things we hold most dear.

Activity
Find a glass candleholder, and devise a way to write on it. You can either stick a piece of paper to it, or use glass pens or paints. Write on it two or three of the things you hold most dear in life. You might pick things that give you value and make you feel safe, such as pride, financial security, reputation, a habit of worrying or a need to be in control. Or you might pick things which are precious and which you find it hard to entrust to God's care, like your spouse, your family, your job or your role at church. Let the Holy Spirit steer you as you choose; remember, you can always add things later.

When you've written on your candleholder, put a candle in it and light it every time you sit down to pray. As you read the writing and watch the flame, let it remind you again of the need to put those precious things back into God's hands, so that he can burn all the more brightly through you.

Talking it

- Have you ever felt like God allowed something to happen to you which felt unfair?
- If Abel's sacrifice was something dear to him, what do you think the modern-day equivalent of Cain's offering might be?
- If sacrificing things we hold dear is difficult and sometimes painful, how can we make it easier for each other to do it? Are there aspects of our community life (in church, for instance) which make it harder to be vulnerable and surrender ourselves to God?

Living it

Practise surrender
Abel brought his sacrifice willingly, without needing to be persuaded or cajoled by God. When you know what it is you have a tendency to hold too tightly, do things which help you to hold it more lightly. For instance, if it's popularity you're clinging to, practise saying or doing things which are good and right, but which might make you less popular. If you're worrying a lot about your children, get yourself into a habit of handing them over to God in prayer every time you think of them. If you're obsessing about money, loosen your grip by giving a bit of it away.

Practise worship
Abel brought his sacrifice because he believed God was worth every bit of the price it cost him. When surrender is painful, there's nothing that soothes that pain like focusing on the one we're surrendering to. Find a list of the names of God (there are plenty online), and choose one name each day. At the start of the day, read the Bible reference where that name appears, and then carry the name with you for the rest of the day. You can write it down and keep it in your pocket, if need be. Develop a habit of thinking about the name you're carrying, what it tells you about God, and how it can strengthen and reassure you as you go about your day.

Faith in company
Genesis 5:21–24

> **Enoch walked faithfully with God; then he was no more, because God took him away.**
> GENESIS 5:24

There's a beautiful scene towards the beginning of Tolkien's *The Lord of the Rings*. It's not one of those scenes where armies march through majestic landscapes, or elves do acrobatics in the trees;

it's much more domesticated. Frodo is sitting with his three hobbit friends by the fire in his cosy new house, musing on the daunting journey he and Samwise are about to undertake, when Merry and Pippin interrupt him to inform him that they're planning to come along too. In response to Frodo's protestations, Merry simply says, 'You can trust us to stick to you through thick and thin – to the bitter end… but you cannot trust us to let you face trouble alone.' Having originally thought he'd have to complete the quest all by himself, Frodo suddenly realises that he will be surrounded by friends who've got his back, and that moment is every bit as powerful as all the impressive battles put together.

The Lord of the Rings is a trilogy, and this particular scene appears near the beginning, in the book called *The Fellowship of the Ring*. 'Fellowship' is one of those words which has become rather quaint and old-fashioned, yet I wonder whether that's because we have lost the art of it. We humans have a fatal addiction to self-sufficiency, and the pressures of modern life don't make it easy to kick that habit. Fellowship is to walk with others: to go at their pace; to value the company just as highly as the destination; to share life together, rather than just getting the job done. Fellowship is time-consuming and, since it involves companionship with others, frequently inconvenient and awkward. Yet every daunting quest is improved by a bit of fellowship.

Having honoured Abel, the writer to the Hebrews moves swiftly on to Enoch: a man who knew a thing or two about fellowship. The only things we know about him are that he walked with God and that he didn't die a natural death. Given the fact that we're still in the early chapters of Genesis here, the news that someone walked with God comes as something of a welcome relief. Adam and Eve had regularly walked with God in the garden of Eden (Genesis 3:8), but they jeopardised that fellowship through pride and disobedience, leaving God no option but to bar them from that paradise. We tend to assume therefore that they forfeited their rights to closeness with God, and that he stopped walking the earth with his creation, but that's not true. God, it seems, has always been willing to walk with anyone who sincerely wants to walk with him.

Our self-sufficiency can cause us to get stuck in a destructive vicious circle. It starts with a belief that we are basically alone in life, and that we need to learn to look after ourselves. It then matures into the conviction that we need to make ourselves worthy by being successful – again, on our own. Then, when we fall short of that success, it hamstrings us with the crippling conviction that our failures make us even more deserving of being left alone. Perhaps that's why Jesus spent three years walking the roads of Palestine with a bunch of distinctly imperfect disciples, because he wanted them to grasp the deep truth that God has not distanced himself from us. He is Immanuel, living proof that God is with us.

> But without faith it is impossible to [walk with God and] please Him, for whoever comes [near] to God must [necessarily] believe that God exists and that He rewards those who [earnestly and diligently] seek Him.
> HEBREWS 11:6 (AMP)

This verse is often quoted in isolation, but in fact it is part of the Enoch story, and that makes a vast difference. When you hear the phrase 'without faith it is impossible to please God', it's easy to feel like you've failed before you've even begun. But when you know that the 'pleasing God' refers back to Enoch, then you can take courage from the way he did faith. If he had pleased God by being a high-flying success story, I'm sure the writer to the Hebrews would have told us. Instead, all we're told is that he pleased God by walking through life in his company. Later in the verse, we are reminded that God rewards those who seek him. Again, the use of the word 'reward' can set us back on the track of thinking we've got to prove ourselves somehow; yet the phrase simply means that if we look for God, we find him. If you get up in the morning and say, 'God, I'd like to walk with you today', then you are immediately in his company. He doesn't play hide-and-seek or wait to see if you're going to score high on the 'being a good Christian' chart first; he is there with you, by his Spirit, enjoying your company.

The story is told of a little girl who was recounting to her parents the things she'd learned about Enoch in her Sunday school session. When it came to explaining how he'd left this mortal life, she scratched her head and thought for a bit, before declaring, 'What happened was that he kept going for walks with God, and one day they walked such a long way that God said it would be too far to go back to Enoch's house, so they might as well go to God's place instead.'

Maybe we'll never get to skip death by walking God home, like Enoch did, but I like to think that walking with God takes us further and further away from our old selves, and nearer and nearer to the hope and fulfilment which God has for us. Enoch's long walk with God took him, step by step, to a whole new life. We can end up making the business of transformation so complicated – believing that we need to undergo umpteen different types of self-improvement programme – yet the thing which transforms us most deeply and most completely is a step-by-step, day-by-day walk in the company of our creator.

This thing called faith has two choices right at its heart: the choice to go beyond ourselves by entrusting to God the things we hold most dear, and the choice to believe that God is the friend beside us who wants to walk with us. When we've made those choices – when we're trusting him and walking with him – then we've set faith in motion, and all sorts of things become possible.

Praying it

One of the last things Jesus said to his disciples was that he no longer called them servants, but friends. Being a servant of Jesus is a very good thing indeed, and it teaches us valuable lessons of humility and obedience, but if we stop there we miss out on the even richer experience of being Jesus' friends.

Activity
Write two lists, one with all the characteristics of a servant you can think of and one with all the characteristics of a friend. Then study them for a while. How do servants differ from friends? Are there things on your 'friend' list which aren't part of your relationship with Jesus yet? When you've given these questions some thought, take some time to pray and ask the Holy Spirit (the Spirit of Jesus) to teach you more about being his friend.

Talking it

- Can you think of a time when you thought you were going to be on your own, but God has surprised you by providing friends and fellowship?
- Do you find it easy to believe that God wants to walk with you? If not, what do you think stops you from believing it?
- How can we help one another not to drift off into self-sufficiency and stubborn independence? What can we do to help each other remember that God is always at our side?

Living it

Prayer-walk your neighbourhood
Why not go on a literal walk with God. Head out into your neighbourhood and walk the streets, asking God to show you things you might not normally notice. As you see and hear things, talk to him about them. You might also want to ask him to talk back to you, telling you the things he wants to do to bless your local community.

Practise the presence
Brother Lawrence was a 17th-century Carmelite monk who wrote a little book about walking with God. Its title is *Practising the Presence of God*, and even if you never read the book, that title carries a wealth of good advice. Our self-sufficient nature means we easily forget that we have a friend at our side, and the only way to solve that is to practise remembering he's there.

Activity

Each time you move to a new place or activity today, stop for a few seconds and deliberately think about the truth that God is with you. When you go into a different room, when you start a conversation, when you begin a task – think about what it means for God's Spirit to be right there alongside your spirit. How might he change the atmosphere of the room you've entered? What might he want to say to the person you're talking to? How might he help in the task you're doing? Get used to including him as you go through your day.

- - - - - - - - -
2
- - - - - - - - -

Noah

By faith Noah, when warned about things not yet seen, in holy fear built an ark to save his family. By his faith he condemned the world and became heir of the righteousness that is in keeping with faith.
HEBREWS 11:7

Walking to a different beat
Genesis 6:1–12

I once followed a gentleman through the ticket barriers at a Tube station in London. He was listening to music on his iPod, and thanks to the volume he had it set to, so was I. He was engrossed in a particularly intense rock number, singing along as he fed his ticket to the machine. On any other occasion, this wouldn't have seemed odd in any way, but on that occasion it sounded completely incongruous, for the simple reason that the station speakers were playing the Spring movement of Vivaldi's *The Four Seasons*. The rest of us were skipping along on cushions of joyful violin twiddles, while he was drilling his way through the city in a thunder of electric guitars.

It's the way of human society to try to make everyone the same shape. We feel uncomfortable with difference, with people who draw attention to themselves by refusing to conform. We use phrases like 'You'll stick out like a sore thumb', as though sticking out is a bad thing. Yet, it is the call of God's people in this world to live differently, especially when society has chosen a shape God never intended it to take. It's our job to live life the way God meant it to be lived, even when everyone around us is living some way completely different.

When you are walking to a particular soundtrack, it dictates everything: your pace, your stride and your whole demeanour. Noah was a man living to a different soundtrack from the world around him. We're told he was a man of integrity in a world where integrity had long since gone out of fashion. He was fair and good in a world where evil seemed to be calling all the shots. He had managed to sidestep all the programming of his society, and he was running his life according to a completely different set of values.

If you're wondering how he did it, the answer is simple, and it's going to sound rather familiar after our encounter with Enoch in the last chapter. We are told that Noah 'walked faithfully with God' (Genesis 6:9).

When you walk beside someone, it is impossible not to hear them. You hear their voice, their footsteps and even their breathing. No matter how loud the crowd gets, you can always hear the one you walk closest to. We can assume, therefore, that walking with God had an impact on Noah's soundtrack. Instead of only hearing the racket of the lawless world in which he lived, he was tuned to God's voice and God's character. The society around him sang a song about God not mattering – maybe even God not existing – but he never allowed that song to become louder than the song God himself was singing to him, and that's why he could live so differently. That's why he could run on a totally different track to those around him, not caring in the least whether he stuck out like a sore thumb. That's why he could build a boat in the middle of a desert, undaunted by incredulity and mockery. That's why he could live the surprising story God had for him. That's why he could literally save the human race.

The truth is, the soundtrack we listen to in life affects the way we move and the way we live. The 'music' in your head affects your walk. If you want to walk differently, the first thing to do is to change the background music. How is your soundtrack today? Are you free to enjoy the strains of the song God sings over you, or do you keep getting interference from the distorted songs of a broken world? Are you hearing the swelling chords of unconditional love, the grace notes of – well – grace, or are they getting drowned out by the discordant jangling of self-doubt? Is it easy to believe that you are treasured by God himself, or is it easier to believe that you're not good enough?

The society Noah lived in was extremely dark. Bible translators have tried various approaches to convey the sheer awfulness of it. The Amplified Bible puts it like this:

> The [population of the] earth was corrupt [absolutely depraved – spiritually and morally putrid] in God's sight, and the land was filled with violence [desecration, infringement, outrage, assault, and lust for power].
> GENESIS 6:11

The Message has this to say:

> God saw that human evil was out of control. People thought evil, imagined evil – evil, evil, evil from morning to night. God was sorry that he had made the human race in the first place; it broke his heart.
> GENESIS 6:5–6

Noah lived with the reality of evil – of a pernicious force working against the good plans God has for his world. We deal today with that same force of evil, though we do so from the far side of the cross of Jesus Christ. We know that evil has been overcome once and for all, but we still feel its dying throes.

Jesus called Satan 'a liar and the father of lies' (John 8:44). It makes sense then that the enemy of our souls would love our internal soundtrack to be filled with lies about us. It serves the purposes of evil for the music in our heads to turn dark sometimes. That's partly why the soundtrack can be so hard to change. We know full well that we're not believing what God's word says about us, but it feels impossibly hard to change the tune.

The good news is that the Holy Spirit has no intention of leaving you to battle alone. He wants to work with you, to help you silence the lies once and for all. In his letter to the Ephesians, Paul mentions that the Holy Spirit has a weapon to put into our hands: 'the sword of the Spirit, which is the word of God' (Ephesians 6:17).

The best defence against the lies of the enemy is the word of God, wielded by the power of the Holy Spirit. It's when we soak in the truth of God's words, and let the Spirit set those words on fire in us, that we begin to let the soundtrack of heaven shape our walk through this fractured, distorted world.

Praying it

One of the best ways to stay tuned to God's voice is to remind yourself of his words. Just like a song that gets stuck in your brain, God's words can circle round and round in your mind, no matter what else is going on in life. Why not get into the habit of choosing a watchword each week throughout the coming year – a word to inspire you and keep you on track when the noise of the world gets a bit too loud.

Activity
Before your week gets underway, set aside some time to listen to God. As you still and focus yourself, ask him to speak to you, and to help you silence any anxiety or negativity which is preoccupying your mind. Next, choose a Bible passage and read it through twice, then spend a few minutes thinking about what you've read. Look for the word, phrase or idea which really stands out to you. It might be a word which describes God's character, or an inspiring phrase about how he wants us to live. Whatever it is, write it down as your

watchword and leave it somewhere where it will catch your eye throughout the week. You could take a photo of it and set it as your wallpaper, for instance; or you could get a pinboard to put your growing collection of watchwords on. As you go about your week, try to keep that watchword in mind wherever you go.

One more thing to note: a watchword isn't a magic word or a mantra. It's the start of a conversation. Our ever-talkative God doesn't just speak his words to stun us into silence. He invites us into an ongoing dialogue with him, known as 'prayer'. As you carry your watchword around with you, keep talking with God about it. Tell him how you feel about it and ask him to teach you more of what it means.

Talking it

- Noah was determined not to be shaped by the society he lived in. In what ways do you think the society you live in might try to shape you?
- Can you think of someone who has lived so differently to the world around them that they've ended up changing it?
- How can we, the church, make the soundtrack of God's love and truth louder, so that more people hear it, and so that it has more of an impact in shaping our society?

Living it

Edifying earworms

Get yourself a good song on the brain. If you're anything like me, there's usually a song going round in your head, and most of the time it's something annoying. Well, believe it or not, we do actually have some say over the earworms we host. Why not start each day singing a song which says the things you want to say about God, about yourself and about the day ahead of you, and then keep singing it, until it's firmly lodged in your brain. That way, you'll have a soundtrack of worship and truth to shape the way you walk through the day.

Proactive encouragement

It's worth remembering that if you struggle to believe that God loves and values you, it is likely that others struggle to believe that about themselves too. Make it your goal this week to encourage at least one person every day by telling them what you like most about them.

Building beginnings
Genesis 6:13–22

A side effect of being a writer is that you get to edit and proofread all kinds of things penned by your friends and family. A few years ago, my mum asked me to look over a precis of her career, which she had been asked to write as she was to be awarded an honorary doctorate for services to education. I was only a couple of sentences in before I entirely forgot the editing work I was meant to be doing, and just got lost in reading about a remarkable woman and her passion for making children's lives better.

What struck me as I read was that my mum knew what she was about. During her undergraduate studies, she became deeply convinced that educating children is all about helping them to know that they have value. From that moment on, wherever she went and whatever she did, whether as a teacher or a head teacher, she kept that conviction at the heart of her work. It wasn't just something she wrote about in reports, it was something she lived out in every relationship, and she still does today. She believes that every human being has intrinsic value, and she has made it her life's work to demonstrate that to everyone she encounters.

The other thing you might also like to know about my mum is that she has never had any desire whatsoever to go abseiling or parascending. Unlike her daughter, she entirely lacks the longing to fly.

For some people, this idea of going 'beyond ourselves', of overstepping our limits and taking great leaps of faith, is not in the least inspiring. Whereas the idea of being a world-changer is exciting to some, it's exhausting to others. Perhaps you're one of those people. Try as you might, you just can't muster up an impressively stunning life goal. You've never wanted to start a global foundation or invent a cure for the common cold, and no one has ever told you that you could be the next Olympic winner or the next president of the USA. If that's you, then relax. You're in Noah's very good company. God had told him to build an ark, but I don't suppose he had any idea quite what that ark would come to mean for humanity. Had you told Noah that the Messiah himself would be talking about him and his boat, thousands of years later, as the ultimate picture of salvation, I suspect he would have been rather sceptical. All he knew was that he had to build a boat to keep himself and his family safe through an impending disaster.

Some world-changers know what they're aiming for from the moment they set out, but most of us don't. Most of us, like Noah and my mum, just start building; we start doing the job that God puts in front of us. For most of us, the hope we're holding tight to is not the strategy to end world poverty or to broker peace in a war zone; it's a simple, uncomplicated plan to protect our loved ones, to serve our communities and to keep valuing everyone we meet.

If that's your hope, don't knock it. The only person who needs to be able to see the big picture from start to finish is God. Noah built his boat, and God saved civilisation. If you build your boat of hope, who knows what God might do with it.

What are you here to build? In truth, what we're called to build is generally closer to home than we think. Noah was asked to build the ark that would save humanity, but that probably wasn't how he saw it when he started out. To him, it was a matter of building a structure out of wood and coating it with pitch. Wood and pitch were ingredients he wouldn't have had too much trouble acquiring, and it is likely he had some idea of how to put them together to make the boat, especially since God had given him all the measurements.

What you've been called to build will be something you can start on with whatever you have to hand. My mum is a natural teacher with a passion for helping people know their value. That's all she needed to start building. Like my mum, you'll find there's something which is very 'you', and which you feel passionately about, and that will be the best place to start.

In our section on Abel, we touched on the subject of sacrifice. Being prepared to sacrifice what we hold dear is indeed central to faith, but the idea has got a little distorted in some people's minds. I have a friend who used to believe that God would always want the opposite to what she wanted. If she admitted to wanting something, then God would immediately ask her to give it up, just to prove her willingness to sacrifice things for him. She honestly believed that God would only ever be completely pleased with her if she managed to give up every single one of her own preferences, and just busy herself doing all the things she hated most. Somehow, for some people, self-denial gets twisted into self-punishment, and they end up bound by the strange and destructive notion that God wants to strip us of everything we love most in life, to make us better people.

Let's get two bits of theology straight right now, shall we? First, God made you. He designed you, with all your qualities and quirks. If you are good at something, it's because he made you to be good at it. Your likes and dislikes, your talents and traits are all part of how he made you, and he never makes a mistake. Second, God loves you. Do you make mistakes? Yes. Does he want to grow you and refine you? Yes. But he is growing you to become more yourself, not less yourself, because he loves who he made you to be. He does not want to erase your personality, he wants to colour it in and bring it to life.

If you want to know where to start building, start with something that is typically 'you'. Perhaps you are a born organiser and you love helping make things happen. Perhaps you're an artist and you love creating things which help people see beauty. Perhaps you have a heart for prayer and you long to see your town transformed by God's love. Perhaps you're a natural at hospitality and you enjoy using your gift to make your street feel like a friendlier place to live. Whatever you're called to build will fit with who you are.

And whatever you're called to build will be something you can start today. Once he'd got his instructions, all Noah had to do was to go and get those first two pieces of wood and nail them together. The rest followed from there. Start doing the thing you love, and step by step, bit by bit, God will use your little acts of faithfulness to build something beautiful.

Every great story has to start somewhere. Even the most heroic deeds start with one small act – whether that's donning your underpants over your trousers or holstering your phaser gun. And those first acts are usually pretty mundane. Maybe it doesn't feel like you can change the world today, but it will be entirely possible for you to get started.

Mother Teresa once said, 'What can you do to promote world peace? Go home and love your family.'

Nowadays Noah is celebrated as a hero whose obedience changed the world. On day one, Noah was just a man who built a boat. Today is the day to start building.

Praying it

For most of us, praying is verbal. It's about putting words together into sentences, putting sentences together into prayers, and then 'saying' those prayers, whether out loud or in our heads. But there's nothing in the Bible to suggest that prayer has to be about words. In fact, our infinitely creative God loves to communicate with us in all kinds of non-verbal ways.

Activity

What are you good at making? Before you close the book in terror, thinking I'm about to ask you to do some origami or crochet, take a deep breath and think wider. 'Making' encompasses a whole host of things: music, art, needlework, cards, cakes, cups of tea; making someone smile, making someone's garden a bit tidier, making someone's car work or making someone feel welcome. Work out what kind of 'making' you're best at, and then think of someone you want to pray for. Instead of praying for them in words, pray for them by making them the thing you're good at. It may not feel like prayer, but if you do it with all your heart, it will be as powerful as any words you've ever prayed.

Talking it

- When you think about people building things for God, is there a particular person who comes to mind? What are they building, how are they building it and how does it fit with their personality, their gifts and their passions?
- On our own it can sometimes be difficult to find out what we're called to build. How could your church better help people to discover what they're called to build?
- Have you ever watched someone undertake something for God which seemed ridiculous or unwise? What happened?

Living it

Who am I?

Have you ever done a personality test? If not, why not give it a try. There are loads out there. None of them are perfect, and the result certainly won't define you, but it will help you to reflect on what kind of person God made you to be: where your strengths and weaknesses lie, and what motivates you in life.

Build in public

I often wonder if Noah ever wished God had given him a building project he could do in secret. It would have been altogether less embarrassing. There's something uncomfortable but healthy about other people knowing we're starting to build. If you know God is asking you to start building something, tell a few people, so that they can encourage you and keep you accountable.

- - - - - - - - -
3
- - - - - - - - -

Abraham

By faith Abraham, when called to go to a place he would later receive as his inheritance, obeyed and went, even though he did not know where he was going. By faith he made his home in the promised land like a stranger in a foreign country; he lived in tents, as did Isaac and Jacob, who were heirs with him of the same promise. For he was looking forward to the city with foundations, whose architect and builder is God.

HEBREWS 11:8–10

Looking with open eyes
Genesis 11:27—12:7

It's the prerogative of every creative person, once in a while, to decide to start again. Whether it's screwing up the paper, squidging down the clay or clicking 'Select all' swiftly followed by 'Delete' in the word processor, most of us will at some moment have felt the frustration that goes with things not turning out how we'd hoped.

There are moments in history when it seems that even God has to start over – moments when humans have managed to steer this world so very far from the course he originally intended for it that he has to take drastic measures to get us back on track. Genesis 11 tells the story of one such reboot moment. A combination of breathtaking pride and mind-boggling technology had led a particular group of human beings to believe that they could, quite literally, build their way up to God. The tower of Babel wasn't just an architectural wonder; it was a statement about humanity's power and God's obsoleteness. Of course, God could just have stormed in and taken possession of the tower, to prove his sovereignty, but that isn't his way. Time and time again through the scriptures we find him refusing to impose his will and his rule, instead preferring to wait for human beings to invite him to take charge. What he does do, however, is to allow us to live the consequences of our errors, and the consequences of this arrogant and ill-conceived plan were that an entire people lost the ability to understand each other, driving each other away until they were scattered across the face of the earth.

God is unimpressed by tall towers and power-hungry men, but he cherishes a fragile, honest hero. Enter Abraham, stage left.

Abraham is a hero of our faith, but not the superhero which we sometimes wish we could be. His story is that of a God who uses fragile, fallible people to catalyse great things. In just a few short verses in Genesis 11, we learn several revealing facts about this man. First, we learn that he had lost a brother. We're not told how Haran died, but since losing a loved one was no easier to handle thousands of years ago than it is today, we can assume that Abraham lived with the pain of bereavement. What's more, he seems to have adopted Haran's son, Lot, into his own family. If you've ever raised stepchildren, you'll know something of the complexities of that particular situation. Third, we discover that Abraham's wife Sarah is unable to have children, something which would have been considered a curse in her day. This bereaved man also had to handle the pain of infertility.

Given all that, you could be forgiven for thinking God should have looked elsewhere for his 'new start' man. But he didn't; there was something in Abraham which made him the perfect pioneer for God's new era, in spite of all his challenges.

> The Lord had said to Abram, 'Go from your country, your people and your father's household to the land I will show you…' The Lord appeared to Abram and said, 'To your offspring I will give this land.' So he built an altar to the Lord, who had appeared to him.
>
> GENESIS 12:1, 7

The first seven verses of Genesis 12 tell of Abraham and his entire household leaving their ancestral home and settling in a foreign land. The account of this monumental event in Abraham's life is bookended by two slightly different renderings of the promise God made to him. In verse 7, after the move has happened, we find the familiar wording, repeated again and again throughout the Pentateuch: God promising to give this new land to Abraham and his descendants. But before he has left his home, the wording is slightly different. In verse 1, instead of telling Abraham he is going to give him the land, he says he is going to show him the land.

Have you ever been in a situation where someone has wanted to show you something new? Perhaps a friend has invited you to watch their favourite film with them, or treated you to some exotic food you've never tasted before. If you have, you'll know how important attitude is. You can look at a new experience with your eyes closed, already assuming you're not going to like whatever it is so you don't even try, or you can look at it with open eyes, embracing it for what it is and enjoying it as much as you can.

God wanted to do a new thing, and he needed a man who would look at that new thing with open eyes. He didn't need someone who would take one look at Canaan and say, 'Very nice, but I think I'll head home again now.' He needed someone who would truly see it and take it to heart.

Abraham saw a beautiful land. Sir Isaac Newton saw an apple fall from a tree. Martin Luther King saw a society where everyone was valued equally. Every new invention, every groundbreaking discovery and every social breakthrough starts with somebody seeing something. The something they see is usually a long way off, and even as they see it, they know it's going to take years, maybe decades or centuries, before the world sees it too. But everything has to start somewhere. If nobody gets excited by that first glimpse, then progress stops happening altogether.

What has God shown you? Do you have a dream which seems impossibly far away? Faith is seeing. It is being able to look way beyond what seems possible now; it is fixing your gaze on a far-away 'what if' and starting to get excited about it.

> What does scripture say? 'Abraham believed God, and it was credited to him as righteousness.'
> ROMANS 4:3

Paul's description of Abraham's faith is simple and life-giving. Abraham opened his eyes and let God show him a new land, and then he believed God. He never saw the fulfilment of the promise, but he believed God. He didn't need to believe in his own ability to make the dream come true; he just had to believe God. It's easy to get stressed about the idea of needing to believe for something, because we think it means psyching up some kind of certainty about what is going to happen and how we're going to make it happen, but faith is just being open-eyed to the possibility of the impossible, to seeing beyond the limitations of how things are now, even if we have no idea quite how God is going to get us from here to there. Faith isn't some mind game where you change things by the sheer power of your thoughts; it's the joyful 'Wow! Yes please!' that bursts from deep inside you when God shows you something wonderful.

Praying it

Our dreams can seem so huge that we get scared to really look at them. God shows us something, and we glance at it, feel a surge of excitement, then look quickly away, for fear we will set our hearts on something too unrealistic. Abraham didn't live to see his descendants occupy the land God had shown him, but God still took him there, because he needed to live in the promise of it.

Activity
Has God given you a dream? Look at it with open eyes. Start by asking the Holy Spirit to help you banish those negative 'It'll never happen' thoughts, and then spend half an hour or so imagining how different things will be when your dream is fulfilled. You might like to write your thoughts down, so you can read them again in the future.

Talking it

- What's your favourite story of a dream coming true?
- Have you ever had a new experience which you were expecting to be negative, but which turned out to be positive?
- People with big dreams are sometimes dismissed or ridiculed for being idealistic. How can we create environments where new ideas are welcomed with open eyes?

Living it

Talk your dreams
Abraham had to take his whole household with him on his dream-pursuing journey. That meant he had to tell at least a few people closest to him what God had shown him. Why not find a couple of people to share your dream with? It's important to choose your co-conspirators wisely, because not everyone will be able to see with open eyes. As you speak it out, it will help to strengthen your own faith.

Move in
What might it mean to start living in your dream, even before it's fulfilled? A few ideas:

- If your dream is to see the crime rate in your local area drop, research which crimes are being committed most and pray for them to stop.
- If you dream of opening a cafe where people can find hope and healing, start praying blessing over every person you make a coffee for.
- If your dream is to see a loved-one get to know Jesus, look out for moments when you see God at work in their lives. You can thank him for those moments, even if they don't even notice them.

Looking up and looking out
Genesis 13:1–18; 15:1–21

I once accompanied a friend on her trip to collect her new glasses from the optician. They were her first pair of varifocals, so the dispensing clerk needed to give her a pep-talk on how to manage the different grades of magnification in different parts of the lenses. I listened with fascination to the warnings about not trying to walk around while looking through the lower half of the lenses (the reading part), because she'd probably end up tripping over things. My guide dog, who lies unobtrusively on the floor, can vouch for the truth of those warnings, because she has stepped on his paws several times since getting the glasses.

It matters where you look. Where you direct your gaze can have a dramatic effect not only on what you see, but on how you see things. Genesis 13 tells the sad story of a man whose faith-filled gaze had slipped. Abraham had moved to the land God had shown him, but family dynamics had become complicated. His relationship with his nephew, Lot, had become so strained that the only solution was for them to go their separate ways. By rights Abraham, the elder of the two men, should have got first choice on where he wanted to live, but instead he let Lot choose. Lot made a strategic choice: he chose the plain, which was fertile and well-populated – ideal for agriculture and trading. Abraham was left with the hill country – a barren and hazardous landscape. In that painful moment, the dream and the promise must have seemed a long way off.

I often imagine Abraham, standing on that barren hill, staring forlornly down at the rocky ground beneath his feet, looking through the magnifying lenses of pain and sorrow and seeing only the raw deal which life had dealt him. Perhaps he berated God for showing him this land, promising him this future, then leaving him to the mercies of life's sharp edges.

> And the Lord said to Abram, after Lot had separated from him: 'Lift your eyes now and look from the place where you are – northward, southward, eastward, and westward; for all the land which you see I give to you and your descendants forever.'
> GENESIS 13:14–15 (NKJV)

In that bleak moment, God intervened to readjust Abraham's gaze. He called him to look up and take in the sweeping vistas around him, because he was going to give him all the land he could see. Had he been down in the plain, he wouldn't have been able to see much of the land, but since he was up in the hills, 'all the land which you see' turned out to be a lot of land!

Our God, the giver of faith, knows that it isn't easy to keep fixing our gaze on the far horizon of his promises. He knows that the pressures of life cause our gaze to slip, and we lose our long-range focus. Instead of dreaming, hoping and believing, we get caught up in worrying, wondering and overthinking. We start trying to problem-solve our way to fullness of life.

Abraham and Sarah were inveterate problem-solvers, and it got them into trouble. They knew God had promised them descendants, so they went about trying to find a way to get Abraham a son, in spite of Sarah's infertility. That ended in Hagar and Ishmael, a slave girl and her baby boy, being thrown out into the desert. On two occasions Abraham was afraid that powerful men would want Sarah for their wife, and would kill him to get her, so he pretended she was his sister. On the first of these occasions (Genesis 12:10–20), he took wealth in exchange for her, and even allowed Pharaoh to sleep with her. When fear comes in, accompanied by the pernicious lie that we need to make things happen in our own strength, then we start to do things which hurt us and those we love.

Faith is not the same lens as fear and problem-solving. If you like, fear and problem-solving are the lower part of the varifocal lens, the part that magnifies tiny details, the part that makes small things big. They have their place: fear is a good lens to look through when you're handling fireworks or an angry lion; problem-solving is a good lens to look through when you're reconciling business accounts or fixing your car. But neither are good lenses to look through when you're believing for something that no amount of human effort alone could ever deliver. If you're fearful, or if you're trying to make things happen in your own strength, then you're looking down and focusing through the magnifier. You need to look up through the part of the lens that deals best with long-range focus, the part that brings far-away things closer. Look down, and you might stumble; look up, and you'll find you can walk with greater confidence.

In spite of his many stumbles, Abraham had several remarkable encounters with God. He lived in a culture where relationship with the divine was highly transactional. You did the right thing by your god and that god would meet your needs in return. You sacrificed the right animals and he or she would send rain on your crops, for example. You did what God required of you, and you hoped that he'd fulfil his end of the bargain. Given Abraham's less-than-ideal behaviour then, God should by rights have wanted nothing to do with him.

Instead, God kept turning up. On one such occasion, in Genesis 15, he asked Abraham to bring parts of some of the animals in his flock – overtones of the costly sacrifice Abel made, perhaps. This would have been familiar territory for Abraham, since it was about paying his dues to God, in return for blessing and prosperity. But what he received that strange night was something rather different. He fell into a deep sleep and awoke to find the presence of God himself walking among the pieces of his livelihood.

Abraham learned that day that God doesn't do transactional. He doesn't make bargains or strike deals. He simply gives us himself. That is a very great reward indeed, and it helps no end with the business of looking up.

I may never have been able to benefit from varifocals, but I did learn a thing or two about looking down and looking up when I was a child. Since I have a tiny amount of sight, I always used to look down, to try to see the thing I was holding or the floor I was walking along. I never bothered looking at people, because I couldn't see their faces anyway, so what was the point. I could glean all I needed from listening to their voices. The loving adults around me had to teach me that it is rude not to look up at someone when they're talking to you. By all means keep an eye on the path ahead, but look up when you're in company.

You are in the very best of company as you walk towards the things you dream of. It's not only polite to look up at the one who walks beside you, it's ultimately better for your health. He will catch your gaze, then focus your vision again on the land he wants to show you.

Praying it

When you're walking towards something that only God can make happen, it stands to reason that prayer will be a vital part of that process. Prayer is the way we connect with the supernatural power of God; if we don't pray about things, we tend to start trying to do them in our own strength.

Activity
Try praying with an 'I can' list and a 'he can' list in front of you. As you pray for a particular topic, think of one thing which you can do

to make a difference to that situation, and write it in the 'I can' list. Then move to the 'he can' list, and note down all the things which are beyond you, and which only God can make happen.

Talking it

- What are the warning signs which alert you to the fact that you've started focusing on fear and problem-solving instead of faith?
- What most helps you look up, to regain perspective and refind hope?
- How can we as church communities refuse the celebrity-culture lie that heroism is about being flawless and unsinkable, and help people grasp the truth that God is looking for human beings, not superheroes?

Living it

Clean lenses
Faith sees impossible things and believes they can happen. Faith sees far-off lands and believes they can be reached. Faith believes God. But the lenses of faith sometimes need cleaning, especially when we've spent too long using the lenses of fear and problem-solving instead. Make a deliberate effort to clean your faith lenses by seeking out the people and things that help you believe: pick up an inspiring biography, read stories of answered prayer, or meet up with someone who helps you look beyond the problems to the possibilities.

Stoke faith
Do you know someone who's focusing more on fear than on faith? Why not send them a message today to remind them that they're not alone, and to encourage them to look up and trust God.

4

Isaac

By faith Isaac blessed Jacob and Esau in regard to their future.
HEBREWS 11:20

The art of consolidation
Genesis 24:1–4; 26:1–6; 28:1–4

> **The essential thing 'in heaven and earth' is that there should be a long obedience in the same direction; there thereby results, and has always resulted in the long run, something which has made life worth living.**
>
> Friedrich Nietzsche

Comparing the patriarchs, Isaac definitely looks the least interesting. Unlike his father, Abraham, and his son, Jacob, he never emigrated to another country, he had just one wife (and no concubines), he got into relatively few scrapes, and God never changed his name. Perhaps, thanks to some of the above, he lived the longest of all three men. When heroes of the faith are discussed, Isaac is often left out. Maybe that's because, after coming dangerously close to being sacrificed during his childhood, his adult life turned out to be comparatively calm. Yet, the writer to the Hebrews deems him worthy of a mention, and so do I. You see, for me, Isaac is a celebration of the noble art of just getting on with it. He received no life-changing promises from the Almighty, and besides some sibling rivalry between his offspring and a few issues with wells, life as a patriarch threw him few curve balls. He just had to continue what had already been started.

One of the things the writer to the Hebrews commends Abraham and Sarah for is the size of their vision. They had dreams that were bigger than themselves – things which could never be realised in their own lifetime, but which they gave themselves for anyway.

> All these people were still living by faith when they died. They did not receive the things promised; they only saw them and welcomed them from a distance, admitting that they were foreigners and strangers on earth. People who say such things show that they are looking for a country of their own. If they had been thinking of the country they had left, they would have had opportunity to return. Instead, they were longing for a better country – a heavenly one. Therefore God is not ashamed to be called their God, for he has prepared a city for them.
> HEBREWS 11:13–16

Abraham didn't just leave home and travel to a new country because he fancied a change of scenery. He travelled because he believed that God had a whole new land for their descendants to inherit. The descendants themselves were something of a mythical concept, given that Sarah was infertile and the land in question was vigorously occupied by other tribes who didn't look like they wanted to move out any time soon, but Abraham obeyed the call anyway. When he died, his number of descendants had risen from zero to a small handful – still a far cry from the number of grains of sand on the average seashore. The only hope Abraham could have of his vision being realised was for his son, Isaac, to carry it on.

Noah and Abraham both got to start something new; Isaac got to develop something that had already been started. He was called to strengthen rather than to initiate, to consolidate rather than to pioneer, and he was extremely successful in fulfilling that call.

The art of consolidation involves two skills: knowing what to hold on to and knowing when to move forward.

Although God had called Abraham to leave his homeland and to move away from his tribe, Abraham knew that God had not called him to abandon his identity and his heritage. His family was not to naturalise in the land of the Canaanites. They were to live there in peace and cooperation, but they were to remain distinct as their own tribe. That's why he took the serious step of requiring his servant to swear an oath that he would find Isaac a wife from Abraham's own tribe (Genesis 24:1–4). And, over a century later, it's why Isaac gave the same command to his own son, Jacob (Genesis 28:1–4).

What are you supposed to be holding on to? In a world where most things are disposable or recyclable, and where new information is constantly flooding our brains and washing out the old, holding on to things can be a tricky business. I used to make 'spiritual resolutions' each year: setting myself a goal to deepen my understanding of a particular aspect of my faith or to grow in a particular character trait, but I gave it up when I suddenly realised, one sunny new year's morning, that I couldn't remember the resolution I'd made the previous year, let alone the ones I'd made in the six preceding years. Life bowls us along at such a rate that we have a tendency to live in the moment, to adapt ourselves to what's going on around us and to forget those old solid things we always meant to hold dear.

In Abraham and Isaac's day, marriage was a matter of identity. To insist on their sons marrying from their own tribe was to say that they would not let go of their identity, no matter where they lived or who they settled among. Are there aspects of your identity that you need to make sure you hold on to? Are there vital, fundamental facets of who you are and what you value which are in danger of losing their colour if you start blending in too much? Are there priorities and habits which all too easily fall away in the helter-skelter of a busy life?

Isaac knew what to hold on to, but he also understood that he needed to move forward. The easiest way to preserve his family's identity would have been to move back home to their tribal lands, but that would have been to undo Abraham's dream and to disobey God's call. Isaac's faith journey was to continue on in his father's footsteps: to deepen his roots in the new land and to prosper there. There was evidently some temptation to strike out in a whole new direction, leaving the land of Canaan and moving to Egypt, which was a better place to be in times of famine, but that too would have been to abandon the vision and disobey the call (Genesis 26:1–6). So he stayed put and kept building the family business, increasing his herds and consolidating his wealth, so that his sons would be even more at home in the land of promise.

Is there a job you need to get on with? Perhaps it feels old and boring, and you're hankering after something new, but you know it's actually the right thing to be doing. Maybe you're feeling inadequate: you've been given the job of carrying someone else's big vision, but you're hesitating because your shoulders don't feel wide enough. Or maybe you've been doing yourself down for not having a shiny new dream of your own. Be encouraged! Consolidating is just as important a job as innovating. Taking something to the next level can be just as rewarding as starting something new. And, if God has called you to carry someone else's vision forward, it's because you will do a better job of it than they would.

Praying it

The regular rhythm of prayer in our lives is one of the things which most helps us to consolidate, because it brings us back, day after day, to the things which matter most – the things we are to hold on to, and the things we are to move towards.

Activity
Choose one item from around your home which signifies something you need to hold on to – perhaps something about your identity

which you need to make sure you don't let go of in the bustle of life. Then choose something which reminds you of the need to move forward or of what you're moving towards. Put both items in the place where you most often have your prayer time (or take a picture of them to carry with you). Each time you pray, look at the first object and think about what you need to keep hold of. Ask the Holy Spirit to help you remember it throughout the day. Then look at the second object and pray that God will give you the strength to take those small but vital 'moving forward' steps.

Talking it

- Through the three generations of Abraham, Isaac and Jacob, God formed the people of Israel. Isaac was the 'middle man' in that story. What are the benefits of being the middle man, and what are the downsides?
- If the art of consolidation can be tricky for an individual, it can be tricky for a church too. How can we help ensure that our churches are holding on to what is essential and precious, but still moving forward?
- Have you ever been asked to carry someone else's vision when you haven't wanted to? How did it feel, what did you do and how did it turn out?

Living it

Consolidation marathons

Do you know someone who's ploughing a long straight line at the moment – someone who's having to just keep on keeping on, even though that obedience is hard and costly? Why not commit to praying for them daily over the coming week, asking God to give them the grace to find new enthusiasm for the old task.

Isaac leaders

Church leaders often carry an 'Isaac' responsibility to consolidate: stepping in to lead a church with an existing vision, understanding what needs holding on to and discerning where they are to help the church move forward. It can be complex and difficult at times. Could you drop your leader a line today to encourage them?

The art of knowing what really matters
Genesis 26:12–25, 27:1–40

A farmer decided to dig a well on his farm. After his first day of digging, he returned, deflated and irritated. 'I've dug down 50 feet today, and still no water!'

His wife was a little surprised at this, since they knew there was an underground water supply on the farm, so she asked him to take her to where he'd been digging. All became clear when he led her around the farm to three completely different digging sites, one where he had dug for 20 feet, one where he had dug for 18 feet, and one where he had dug for 12 feet.

'See!' he said. 'No water anywhere on this wretched farm!'

'I think, dear,' she said, trying not to sound too patronising, 'that you were meant to dig all the 50 feet in the same place.'

The digging of wells is not the job for a pioneer who likes to keep moving on to something new. The digging of wells is a job for a patient consolidator, and Isaac was a man who did well at digging wells.

In Isaac's day, the business of cattle-farming in the Negev desert depended on wells. If you had a well, you could keep your animals watered, and you could even grow food for them. Without a well, you were at the mercy of the elements. The best way to attack a cattle-herder then was to pollute or block up his wells, and that's what Isaac's Philistine neighbours did. Isaac could have been forgiven for losing his temper and retaliating, but he was the ultimate pragmatist. He knew when a thing wasn't worth fighting over – even something as important as a well.

Sometimes letting go is the right thing to do. We humans are good at wasting our time and energy trying to hold on to the wrong things. We do it for all kinds of reasons: we hold on to things because they make us feel good, or because we want to be proved right, or because we don't think we can cope without them. But in the end, the holding on can stop us moving forward. Isaac could have stayed and fought for every single well the Philistines blocked up, but he knew that would trap him in the stalemate of turf wars, so he just let them go.

How do we let go of things that seem as vital to us as wells? There's much wisdom in Isaac's approach.

First, he named the wells he was letting go of. The two wells we read about in Genesis 26:20–21 became places of conflict with the Philistines, so he named them 'Dispute' and 'Opposition'. Why name them at all? Surely the best thing would have been to put them behind him and forget about them. When things in our lives become contentious, it's all too easy to want to be rid of them as quickly as possible. Have you ever seen a toddler lose the battle over keeping hold of a toy when it's time to put it away? All too often, at the point of inevitable surrender, the toy gets flung into the toy box in a fit of rage, as though it's the most hated object in the world. To name something is to acknowledge it, to say it mattered, to say it was beautiful, to say it was painful. To name something is to face up to it in a whole and mature way, even though it hurts to do so and we'd rather forget it.

And having named those places of failure and loss, Isaac just dug a new well. You see, he was a seasoned stockman. He knew there was more water to be had, and he knew that his God had promised to supply his needs in that land. So he stepped out in faith and trust, and kept digging wells until he found the one that no one would contest. He called it 'Rehoboth', which means 'room' or 'spacious place' (Genesis 26:22).

There is a Rehoboth for you. Somewhere beyond the frenzied fighting and the frantic clinging on, there is a place where there is space to breathe. The trouble is, it may just mean letting go, even though every instinct in you is telling you not to give up the fight. Name this place, then put it behind you and look for a new place to dig.

If you're a visionary, it can be especially hard to let go and accept something which seems, at first glance, to be less perfect than what you'd hoped for. If that's you, then you're in good company with Isaac. It wasn't just wells that got complicated for him, it was sons too. He loved his first-born son, Esau, and was ready to pass Abraham's sacred covenant blessing on to him at his death, but instead he got duped by his wife and his younger son and ended up passing it on to Jacob by mistake (Genesis 27:1–40). When Isaac found out what had happened, he was deeply distressed. The blessing couldn't be undone, and things weren't how he'd wanted them to end up. Yet, ever the pragmatist, he simply found a workaround. He found a new and different blessing for Esau. And in the end it's this that the writer to the Hebrews celebrates: not the wells, the prosperity or the business of marrying the right woman – no, it's the practical and gracious choice to make the best of a bad situation by blessing both sons into a hope-filled future.

Faith is sometimes about being handed the title deed to a perfect dream, and sometimes it's about making the best of it when the documents get muddled up in the post and we end up custodians of a dream which isn't quite as we'd hoped it would be. Whichever it is, God is still God, and if we let him, he will work it all out in the end. If we can let go, and let him do his work, we will find that the endless creativity of his grace can sustain any amount of human error, so long as we keep trusting him.

There's one more aspect of Isaac's story which I find heartening: he didn't seem to have half as many dramatic encounters with God as Abraham did. Most of Isaac's encounters with God seem to have been moments of reassurance and reaffirmation of the promises he'd made to Abraham – a kind of 'as you were' to encourage him to keep going. Abraham's encounters with God were awe-inspiring, but Isaac's had a practical, everyday feel to them. On one occasion, after all the contentious well-digging, he found himself at Beersheba, where, after a comforting visit from the Almighty, we are told he pitched his tent, built an altar and dug a well. Those three acts say it all. Worship was real and deep in Isaac's life, but it happened in the midst of the home-making and the well-digging.

When our call is to consolidate, we need to be able to find God in the everyday. When Nietzsche's 'long obedience in the same direction' feels more akin to what we're living than the excitement of mountain-top experiences and thrilling adventures, there is something deeply reassuring about knowing that our God is as real and present in the ordinary, everyday things of life as he is in the dramatic events which change the course of history.

Praying it

The Hebrew tradition of naming wasn't just about giving something a handy title for reference. To name something, in Isaac's culture, was to speak the truth about it – as much truth as you could cram into one word or phrase. Naming was an emotional business!

Activity
Is there something you know you need to let go of? Before you do, take some time in prayer to name it before God. Call it what it is; say as much about it as you can to him; admit how much it means to you and how much letting go of it will hurt. Then, when you've done that, put it gently into his hands. Later, if you feel those pangs of pain at letting go, remind yourself that it's in his hands.

Talking it

- Have you ever given something up, even though it seemed like madness at the time? What made you do it and how did it turn out?
- It can be hard to know what to let go of and what to hold on to or fight for. What are your tips for telling the difference?
- Disputes are a regular cause of churches getting stuck, failing to grow and even falling apart. What can we do to prevent the kind of disputes that stop us moving forward, and how can we help resolve them when they happen?

Living it

Find your Rehoboth
Physical places can be excellent ways to help us focus on spiritual truths. Is there a place which feels like a Rehoboth well for you: a spacious place where you feel free and peaceful. Why not make time to visit it sometime soon?

Lend a digging hand
Do you know someone who has just had to let go of something and needs to move on. Is there something practical you can do to help them start digging their new well today?

5

Jacob

By faith Jacob, when he was dying, blessed each of Joseph's sons, and worshipped as he leaned on the top of his staff.
HEBREWS 11:21

What's in a name?
Genesis 25:19–34; 32:22–32

The things people say about us can be tremendously powerful. If they're positive, they can encourage us and spur us on, but if they're negative, they can do great damage.

Jacob had an unfortunate start in life. He came out of the womb holding his older brother's heel, which is roughly what the name 'Jacob' means, but in the Hebrew language grasping the heel is also an idiom meaning a con-artist. It's hard to understand why any parent would choose such a name for their child, especially in a culture where name-giving was so important. As we learned from Isaac's story, names weren't just given as codes of reference, they were given to define. Your name wasn't just the word you were known by, it was the summation of who you were.

Perhaps the reasons for Jacob's unfortunate naming lie in the way that same culture viewed childbirth. In our modern era of medical knowledge, we understand much about what happens to babies while they're in the womb and when they're being born. But in a culture thousands of years before ultrasounds and pregnancy-progress books, the things that happened before, during and after childbirth were surrounded by far more superstition than science. Rebekah had felt a lot of uncomfortable foetal movement, so she prayed about it and received a rather mysterious answer from God about some kind of future turbulence between her offspring (Genesis 25:22–23). Then the babies were born, and the sight of Jacob holding his brother's heel would have been seen as an omen. In the belief systems of the time (even among God's covenant people), omens mattered; they told you what was going to happen and how things would be. The way Jacob was born would have been seen as indicative of the way he would live.

Our culture may be different when it comes to naming, but names still hold immense power. I remember the day we did name-meanings in school, and someone told me that, since they couldn't find my name on any of their lists, it must be derived from Linda, which, they informed me, meant snake-like. I was horrified and mortified! Everyone else had names meaning pretty things like princess and gift, whereas I was labelled slimy and scaly.

(If your name is Linda, I should reassure you here that, though there is a small amount of evidence to suggest that the name has links to a word meaning snake in old Germanic languages, it is far more likely to derive from the German word for soft or tender and the Spanish word for beautiful.)

In truth, it's rarely our given names that are such an issue nowadays. Most parents are more tactful when naming their children than Jacob's parents were. For us, it's more likely to be the nicknames that cause problems. They may be meant with great affection, but they can be immensely damaging if we doubt for a single second whether the one speaking them loves us. My dad and brother have, over the years, caused great consternation by their insistence on referring to me as 'blind bat'. I can safely say I have never received those words as anything but the height of affection and admiration (after all, I'd like to see them try to do life without eyesight!), but I am fully aware that, should I ever for a moment have felt less than loved by them, that name could have become a painful insult.

What have people named you? Perhaps it's a nickname that you've taken to heart or something people have said about you so often that it has taken up residence in your identity. Hopefully it's something good, like 'beautiful', 'precious' or 'strong', but perhaps you've been called 'useless', 'thick' or 'pushy' – something that has caused you to doubt your own worth. It's time to lose the bad names.

Like his grandfather Abraham, Jacob was given a new name by God. In Abraham's case, the renaming seemed to be a rather peaceful, matter-of-fact business. For Jacob, however, it happened during one of the most terrifying nights of his life, as he prepared to meet Esau, his brother and lifelong enemy, and it came as the result of a messy wrestling match with a mysterious being. Whole books have been written on who Jacob wrestled with and why, and I'm not even going to try to guess at the answers. I'm just going to suggest that we stop for a moment and ponder that image of a person wrestling through the darkness of the night – wrestling from fear of what's to come; wrestling from shame over the wrong they've done; wrestling from anger at how life has treated them; wrestling in desperation for some kind of new and different future. That night was a turning point for Jacob. Yes, he received a new name, but he also changed. He lived differently from that moment on, and that was his choice. No new name, no matter how inspiring, could make that happen.

Jacob wasn't a robot, preprogrammed to follow a path of faith that would bring his family one generation closer to the fulfilment of God's promises for them. He was a man who had every right to carve out his own path and work out his own relationship with the God of his forefathers. He was what you might call 'non-compliant': where others could accept, Jacob needed to question; where others could follow the rules, Jacob needed to rearrange the rule book; where others could submit easily, Jacob needed to grapple. But

God loved him just the way he'd made him, and he even celebrated that combative nature by giving him the name Israel, which means 'contended with God'.

One of the interesting things about the wrestling was just how evenly matched the two fighters were. If it was God, wouldn't he have just knocked Jacob out with one unbeatable blow, to prove his supremacy? Jacob learned that night that the God who walks with us is not interested in overpowering us. He doesn't fear us and he doesn't need to prove himself stronger. If we need to wrestle, he'll match us. If we need to contend, he'll contend with us. The only thing he won't do is leave us to face a terrifying night alone.

Early in his career, Walt Disney was fired by a newspaper editor who said Disney 'lacked imagination and had no good ideas'. He and Jacob had one thing in common: they didn't let the things said about them define their identity or their future. Disney went on to use his imagination to bring joy to millions. Jacob went on to become a man of integrity, staying faithful to the covenant he had inherited. You may have started life with a particular name, or you may have picked up descriptors along the way which have been destructive, but those names do not define you, and they certainly don't limit what you will be and do in the years to come.

Praying it

Your name is a part of your official identity. If you want to change it, you need a legally binding document to do so. That document, called a deed poll, uses some powerful language to express what it means to get rid of one name and to take up another.

Activity
What is the most negative word or nickname you've been known by, over the years? And what is the positive, beautiful, life-giving name you want to be known by? Write these two down, and then look up the official wording of the name-change deed poll. Read it out loud,

inserting the two names you've written down, as appropriate. It may not feel like prayer, but don't be fooled by feelings. It is a powerful, prayerful and transformational thing to do.

Talking it

- Do you know what your birth name means? Do you like it, or do you wish you'd been called something else?
- Have you ever met someone who often uses negative-sounding names to describe themselves? Have you ever challenged them or helped them find kinder words to use?
- Many families still opt to have their children christened or dedicated in church. What could we do to make those naming ceremonies even more of a blessing and a moment of significance in the family's life?

Living it

Living up to a name
Names and behaviours easily get locked together. Someone who's always been told they're shy may tend to avoid meeting new people, because they assume they're no good at it. Making a small change in behaviour sometimes helps break the power of an old name. What behaviour do you need to change, to help you part company with an old name, or live up to a new one? Don't be too hard on yourself; behaviour change takes time and practice.

The power of naming
How careful are you when you talk about other people? Do you slip into calling them the same sort of things everyone else is calling them? As you speak about people this week, think about what words you are using to describe them. Don't be afraid to buck the trend and speak positive things over them, and don't be afraid to challenge others when they use negative or unkind words about people.

Scandalous grace
Genesis 28:10–22; 48:1–22

If you're the fair-minded sort, the Old Testament can be a frustrating place to be. Just when you think you've worked out how things should be done and who should be blessed, you read on a bit further and realise that, somewhere along the way, God seems to have changed the rules.

Where are we up to so far, then, in this story of the patriarchs? Abraham moved his family to a new land, in obedience to God's call. Isaac lived on in that legacy, establishing the family line in the new land, and looking ever forward to the day when his descendants would fill it and occupy it. Then Jacob came along, stole the birthright, with all its responsibilities to live out Abraham's covenant and pursue his dream, and what did he do? He promptly went back to Abraham's homeland for 20 years! It's true that Isaac had told him to go, because he wanted him to take a wife from among his own people, but he surely can't have meant Jacob to stay there for two decades. What about the commitment to life in the new land?

I'll stop recounting the story there, because it has a habit of raising my blood pressure. Read Genesis 29—31. It's a pretty messy tale of deception, manipulation, jealousy and power games. You see, whether Jacob really had been born dishonest or whether he just lived up to that identity because of the name others had given him, the truth is that he lived much of his life according to a moral compass which most of us would consider distinctly wonky.

And yet, God confirmed his covenant with him again and again. God blessed him again and again. God drew near to him in the most extraordinary encounters. Abraham met God several times and so did Isaac, but there is a different quality to Jacob's meetings with the Almighty. His father and grandfather talked with God, but Jacob saw the very stairway to his home. God appeared to Abraham and Isaac, but he touched Jacob.

God encourages us, even commands us, to live lives that are upright and good, but he reserves the right to show up wherever he likes, whenever he likes, and however deserving or undeserving his audience may be. The Bible makes it clear that being visited by God is not dependent on us living the perfect life. It is dependent on the God of grace choosing to come to us, even when we don't deserve it.

Perhaps that is the key to Jacob's experience of God. Perhaps it was his own awareness of his habitual sin that made him more deeply grateful for God's love. Towards the end of his life, he described God as:

> 'The God who has been my shepherd all my life to this day, the Angel who has delivered me from all harm.'
> GENESIS 48:15–16

In fact, Jacob is the first person in scripture to use that beautiful name 'shepherd' to describe what it felt like to be cared for by God. He messed up many times along the way, but he knew he was deeply loved.

Have you been disqualifying yourself from meeting with God because you've messed up? Have you been assuming that he wouldn't want to show you the depth of his love for you because you have failed all the worthiness tests? If that's you, then Jacob has some news for you. It's the most messed-up messers-up who most need God to show up – and he does.

In theory, we know about grace, and yet we still fall into the trap of concluding that if we get everything right, step out boldly in faith and do our very best, then God's plans will be more likely to succeed than if we mess up and opt out. Jacob is evidence enough that God has countless ways of getting his promises and his people back on track. Had Jacob insisted on staying with his father-in-law, perhaps God would have had to find someone else to pursue the vision of the new land, but in the end grace changed the conclusion to Jacob's story. After his 20-year detour, he did finally settle in the land God had given to his family line, and he raised twelve sons there. He was a long way from perfect, but he still played a vital part in God's redemption plan.

If we're going to grasp this lifestyle called faith, we're going to have to get to grips with grace too; otherwise we're going to get caught up in yet another version of works – earning our way into God's good books by developing some top-grade faith. We've seen already that faith has a proactive element: faith is sacrificing; faith is walking with God, and seeing the possibilities beyond the horizon of our humanness; faith is building and consolidating. But faith is also reminding ourselves that God is in charge, and that he has ultimate responsibility for fulfilling his promises. Sometimes, our greatest act of faith is simply to give him our blemished, broken selves, so that grace can work its wonders in us.

An event near the end of Jacob's life really sums up this message of scandalous grace. Of the many strange and remarkable things that happened in Jacob's life, it's this event which the writer to the Hebrews chooses to celebrate as his greatest act of faith. Joseph heard that his father was dying, and decided to take his sons to be blessed by their grandfather. Jacob, still thwarting convention, even on his deathbed, did two surprising things.

First, he adopted the boys as his own sons. Yes, it was that simple in those days! He spoke a word, and suddenly they had equal status with their father and all their uncles, and they became coheirs to everything he owned. Then, he blessed each one, but he crossed his hands over, so that Ephraim (the younger one) received the blessing of the firstborn and Manasseh (the elder one) received the blessing of the second-born. Was he remembering the day he himself had received the blessing of the firstborn? It's impossible to say, except that we know he was acting on a word from God. Somehow, some strange work of divine grace was underway.

Picture it: Jacob's arms in a cross-shape; an instant adoption into sonship; extravagant and unfair blessings landing on the least-deserving. This was one of those moments when a man's simple actions told a story far bigger than he could ever have imagined. Jacob was foreshadowing another cross, another moment of adoption and another cascade of scandalous grace on another undeserving head – on my head and on your head.

We don't deserve grace. We don't deserve to meet with God – to hear him, to know him, to sense his touch. Any time we start to tell ourselves that we are getting it right, that we are doing the things that will make him want to draw near to us, we need to stop and remember the cross. We learned from Abel's story that faith involves sacrificing the things we hold most dear, but no sacrifice we ever make will match the one he made. It's him who wants to adopt us into his family. It's his sacrifice that makes us worthy to receive those extravagant blessings. It's his choice to make us part of his story to transform his world.

Sometimes faith is having a dream. Sometimes it's being obedient and working hard. And sometimes faith is believing that, against all the odds and in spite of everything that's gone wrong, you're one of the family.

Praying it

Scandalous grace can never be fully absorbed by our minds alone. It needs to touch our emotions, and that means you might need to go 'beyond words'.

Activity
Rather than trying to pray wordy prayers about God's grace, why not spend some time doing something which stirs your soul. You might listen to music, go for a walk somewhere beautiful, or look at something that takes your breath away. As you do, let the truth of grace soak into your being.

Talking it

- Have you ever been surprised by God showing up when you didn't think you deserved it?
- Scandalous grace offends people, because it often looks like others are prospering while they themselves are struggling. How do we help those who feel God has treated them unfairly?
- How do we find the balance of celebrating God's grace in people's lives, without seeming to condone behaviours we believe to be wrong?

Living it

Cross-spotting
The cross is one of the simplest shapes in all of creation, and you'd be surprised where it turns up. Look out for crosses this week: in the clouds, in man-made structures, on paper, on the computer screen. Every time you see one, stop for a moment to thank God for the cross.

Noticing the unnoticed
Feeling disqualified is a crushing experience. Look out for people around your community who feel disqualified: unworthy of kindness, excluded by society because they don't fit, overlooked because they're too shy, or just plain ignored by everyone who walks past. Will you take a moment to notice them and to stop and talk to them? You may be the way God wants to tell them today that they matter. It may be through you that he wants to meet with them.

6

Joseph

By faith Joseph, when his end was near, spoke about the exodus of the Israelites from Egypt and gave instructions concerning the burial of his bones.

HEBREWS 11:22

Route recalculation
Genesis 37:1–6; 39:1–23

I've never been that good at setting life goals, but I've always had a rough idea of where I'm heading. The plan, such as it was, was simple: I'd get my degree, maybe do a master's, then find some work which would be both fulfilling and challenging. Of course, there would be marriage and children, and no shortage of family Labradors, since I'd probably need a few guide dogs along the way. Despite loving the stories of the heroes, I've never much wanted to travel the world or settle in distant lands, so my tidy little life-map suited me fine.

It was after about eight years of 'trying for a family' that I started to wonder whether God might be recalculating the route.

I have a lot of sympathy for people who rail against the idea of there being a Plan A and a Plan B for our lives. I wholeheartedly agree that God is far too brilliant to be restricted by our understanding of best and second best. But for this section of the story, please bear with me while I talk in those terms. To me, being unable to conceive felt like a disastrous and heartbreaking second best. I threw myself wholeheartedly into all the other wonderful things in my life, but I couldn't bring myself to accept that this was how it was always meant to be.

It's at moments like those that I'm most glad of heroes like Joseph. When he was a boy, Joseph was a dreamer. The Bible doesn't tell us exactly what he thought about the generations-long faith story which he and his family were involved in, but given that he didn't seem to have much trouble believing that he, second-youngest son of the family, could one day be a ruler and clan chief, we can assume he had a natural bent for dreaming big. And whatever his dreams involved, they definitely didn't involve being threatened with death, sold into slavery, convicted of a crime he didn't commit and thrown into prison for several years. That was a devastating run of second bests.

To have hopes and dreams is also to risk disappointment. There's always the option of ditching the hopes and dreams – taking the 'what will be will be' approach, where you avoid setting your hopes on anything, accept everything as though it was always meant to be and thus avoid any disappointment – but it's hard to read the scriptures and stick to that philosophy. Our Hebrews 11 heroes are just some examples of the hundreds of stories in the Bible where people hoped, believed, prayed and worked to see dreams come true.

So what does faith look like when the dreams just won't come true? How do we weather the route recalculations without losing heart and losing hope?

The Genesis storyteller makes much of Joseph's character. Perhaps that's because he stands in stark contrast to his father, Jacob. Joseph may well have been immature and boastful as a boy, but he grew into a man of honesty and integrity who wouldn't have dreamed of cheating on his master or scamming people for what he could get out of them. He was miles from home, in a foreign culture with unfamiliar values and customs, but he stayed true to his own light. He lived the way he believed his God wanted him to live, and he didn't compromise.

Disappointment can so easily turn to pointlessness. If we're a million miles from where we want to be going in life, we start to ask what's the point. What's the point of doing our best? What's the point of living with integrity? We begin to harden ourselves, toughening our emotional skin against the pain of the knock-backs, and in time we can end up hardening ourselves against God himself. We close our hearts and keep our distance from him because, after all, isn't it his fault we're on to Plan B in the first place? If he wanted to, he could put us back on the road we've always wanted to be on, but he's chosen not to.

Joseph wasn't where he wanted to be. His father, Jacob, had ended up in bad places by his own wrong choices, but Joseph ended up in a bad place because of someone else's wrong choice. Jacob's Plan B was self-inflicted, whereas Joseph's was the result of circumstances beyond his control.

If that's your story at the moment, you'll be encouraged by a strange little Bible equation. The phrase 'the Lord was with' is a familiar one from our reading of the Old Testament; yet it's interesting that it is rarely applied to Abraham, Isaac or Jacob, whereas it is used four times to describe Joseph. I don't suppose for a minute that God wasn't with the others; we've seen that his presence was a regular feature in their lives. But it is as though the narrator wants us to know that Joseph's painful Plan B was absolutely full of God. God hadn't made it happen – it was Joseph's brothers who had made it happen by their abusive behaviour – but God was right there in it. He didn't just turn up in the defining moments, speak a timely word, and then leave him to get on with it. God was with him. God was with him in the pit where he'd been left to die; God was with him in that shame-filled moment of sexual manipulation in Potiphar's house; God was with him through the long, dark years in prison.

We know little of what God said to Joseph as they walked that recalculated route together. His appearances to Abraham, Isaac and Jacob tended to involve great pronouncements, but there's none of that in Joseph's story. In the end, Joseph's Plan B turned out to be the saving of his whole family line from starvation, but God didn't tell him that. There was no 'this is how it's all going to work out for good in the end'. There was just the Lord walking with him every step of the way.

God may allow your route to be recalculated, but he will always be with you. You may not get the answers to your prayers, but you will always have the company of the one who has your very best interests at heart.

I wish I could say I've already cracked this one. The truth is that I'm still working on it. Some days I feel able to submit graciously to the route recalculation. Some days I even feel happy and at peace, enjoying the life I have, trusting God with my future. Then there are the days when I feel like screaming at the heavenly sat nav, 'I don't want an alternate route. I want the route I chose in the first place!'

On those days, it is harder to pray, harder to trust and harder to enjoy his company. But he is no less present with me on those days than on the good days. He has promised, over and over again in his word, that he will never leave me nor abandon me. He walks beside me, whether I feel like talking to him or not. He may not give me all the answers, but he gives me himself and even on my worst days, I know that that is a gift beyond compare.

Praying it

Reflection is an important spiritual discipline: looking back over our lives, being honest about the paths we wish we hadn't had to take and noticing how God has led us to where we are today.

Activity

Draw two road maps of your life: one showing the route you would like to have taken and one showing the route you have actually taken. Be honest about the differences – the things you'd hoped to do but haven't done; the events you've lived through which you never imagined would ever happen; the good things you never dreamed you'd experience. As you mark each event, keep repeating the phrase 'the Lord was with me'.

Talking it

- Have you known a time when life has taken a different route to the one you wanted? What do you remember most about that time?
- Is there a particular truth – a saying or a Bible verse, perhaps – which has helped you cope with disappointment?
- Some people find praying with others particularly painful when they've experienced disappointment. Are there things we can do, as churches, to make sure our corporate prayer times give space for the pain of disappointment, as well as the joy of dreaming?

Living it

Perspective matters

Perspective is vital. For most of us, the disappointment we feel is related to one particular area of life, and yet it can feel as though it eclipses everything else. Take time this week to appreciate the things that are good: the areas of your life where you feel fulfilled, the people who bring you joy and the prayers which have been answered.

Integrity matters

Joseph walked his recalculated route with integrity. Are you aware of areas where you're letting standards slip because you're not where you want to be? Make a conscious choice this week to be true to yourself and to God, even in those areas where life is not as you'd like it to be.

Detours, diversions and dead ends
Genesis 41:50–52; 50:1–26

This has been one of those weeks where I've coped less graciously with the route recalculations in our journey towards having children. I'm not sure why – maybe friends announcing pregnancies or that feeling of life moving inexorably forward without me really knowing what I'm here for, if not to be a mum. I'll stop there, otherwise my local computer repair shop might be handling its first case of tear-drenched laptop.

Yesterday morning, I was making my usual choice of which jewellery to wear when I suddenly had a mini meltdown. I have two necklaces which I use for everyday: one with a flower on it and one which has a heart-shaped pendant with 'nothing is impossible with God' embossed on it. The heart-shaped one was a birthday gift from my brother and his family, who know the journey I've been on, and I love it because it says something which I believe and which I want to live by. Yesterday was not a day for feeling full of faith, though, and I couldn't bring myself to wear it, so I reached for the flower instead. Annoyingly, the chain had got knotted and I couldn't untangle it without being late for a prayer meeting, so I grudgingly picked up the 'nothing is impossible' pendant and hung it round my neck. I don't think I have ever worn it and believed it less.

Joseph was a young man of integrity who remained unstintingly faithful to God, even though his road took a very different direction to the one he would have imagined. Yet even Joseph had dark days when he must have wondered if he could keep believing. While he was in prison, he made the costly choice to use his gift of dream interpretation to help two men who were troubled. Having done his best for them, and having been assured that they would speak well of him to the powers that be, the baker promptly got executed and the cupbearer forgot all about him. He languished in prison another two years (Genesis 40:23—41:1).

When our circumstances seem bleak, it can be hard to believe that God's power and goodness haven't changed. We get stuck in a kind of logic: if we've prayed for something and the answer has come quickly, then it must have been an easy thing for God to do, whereas if we've been praying for years and it still hasn't happened, then God must somehow be finding it more difficult. That's partly why it can be so hard to keep believing. I hung that necklace around my neck thinking: if God could give us a family, surely he would have done it by now; since he hasn't, it must be too difficult for him; and if it's too difficult for him, then what hope is there?

Perhaps Joseph's faith took a similar slide. Perhaps, when he first arrived at Potiphar's house, he expected God to intervene quickly to rescue him, but by the time he'd been forgotten in the depths of an Egyptian prison, he started to wonder whether this situation might actually be too difficult even for God.

God does not change. His power and his love don't wax and wane. The speed at which he works may change, the way he does things may change, but his love for you and his ability to do miracles in your life never change. There is no human circumstance that can make God less able or less powerful, and there is nothing you can do that will make him less inclined to love you absolutely.

My own story hasn't finished yet, but I take heart from Joseph's: at the right time, and in his perfect way, God turned Joseph's situation from hopelessness to fulfilment.

Being someone who teaches on prayer, one of the questions I am most often asked is: 'How do you know when to stop praying for something?' It is a question which had resonance in Joseph's life. There came a moment when he had to embrace the unplanned route and let it lead him somewhere he'd never imagined going. He had dreamed of leadership, but I am pretty sure he wasn't thinking of becoming prime minister of Egypt. In his accepting of this different future, there was a letting go of the old hopes and the old prayers. He named his first son Manasseh, which sounds like the Hebrew word for 'forget':

> 'It is because God has made me forget all my trouble and all my father's household.'
> GENESIS 41:51

He named his second son Ephraim, which sounds like the Hebrew for 'twice fruitful'. In Egypt, that place of bitter disappointment, God gave him a double portion of blessing.

There are no easy answers for knowing when to alter or let go of a prayer you've prayed for years. It is a deeply personal matter which can only truly be worked out between you and God. I often liken it to trying on clothing. Every so often, I will 'try on' a different answer to the one I'm longing for. In my case, I will 'try on' the idea of adoption or of never having children. At the moment, though my logical brain can see the benefits and blessings in each of those alternatives, my heart knows neither option quite fits me yet. Maybe one of them will, one day, but for the moment the prayer my heart always returns to, the prayer which is deepest in me, the only prayer that feels like it 'fits', is the prayer to conceive and give birth to our own child. And so I keep praying that prayer.

Letting go of a prayer that you've been praying is painful. After years of not getting the answer you have hoped for, it is the final, profound acceptance that it is time to stop pursuing that long-held dream. It is a fragile, vulnerable time, and if we are going to come through it with our faith intact we need to hang on to a truth that Joseph discovered. As his brothers begged his forgiveness, Joseph said:

> 'You intended to harm me, but God intended it for good to accomplish what is now being done, the saving of many lives.'
> GENESIS 50:20

If God allows a detour, a diversion or even a dead end, it is because he can use it to do something good. He only ever has one intention in mind for you: pure and ultimate good. It may not feel good, but by the work of his unchanging love and power he will work even the worst things for good in your life, if you let him.

It's interesting that Joseph's mention in the Hebrews 11 hall of heroes has nothing to do with any of the things we've talked about so far. His one sentence has nothing to do with surviving jail or averting famine in Egypt. It has to do with him wanting his children to return his bones to Canaan, after his death. Even when his own life took a monumental detour, he didn't lose sight of God's promise to give the land of Canaan to Abraham's descendants. Even though he had to let go of the longing to be there himself, he didn't let his own disappointment stop him believing for better things for the future of his family.

Faith sometimes means giving up on a prayer you've been praying, but it never means giving up hope. Hope isn't the product of answered prayer. It's an ancient, indestructible gift given to us by the one who is weaving all things together into the perfect happy ending.

Praying it

Our prayers aren't just the words we say or the thoughts we think; they are the deep desires within our hearts. Sometimes it's possible to be praying one prayer with our lips, and a completely different prayer in our hearts.

Activity
As you pray today, notice your heart-prayers and your head-prayers. Choose something to pray for, and then see if there are any differences between what your head knows you should be praying and what your heart is actually praying. This isn't about changing your prayers to improve them; it's about being honest and handing your contradictions over to the God who loves you and knows what's best.

Talking it

- Have you ever let go of a long-held dream? How did you know it was time to let go?
- Have you ever thought you'd reached a dead end, but found you'd been given a double blessing instead?
- Have you ever prayed with someone for something which you, in all honesty, didn't have faith for? How did you handle the difference between their expectations and yours?

Living it

Wearing the promises

There's an ancient Jewish tradition of wearing God's word about your person. Is there a promise from scripture which is precious to you, and which you know you need to hold on to, even when you don't think you believe it any more? Why not find a way of wearing it? You could have it engraved on something or just buy an item of jewellery or clothing which symbolises it. Choose to wear it on the days when you are struggling to believe.

Friends on the detour

When faith seems fragile, it can help to know that others are praying with you. Is there someone you know who feels like life has taken a detour at the moment? Why not drop them a line to let them know you're praying for them?

7

Moses

By faith Moses, when he had grown up, refused to be known as the son of Pharaoh's daughter. He chose to be ill-treated along with the people of God rather than to enjoy the fleeting pleasures of sin… By faith he left Egypt, not fearing the king's anger; he persevered because he saw him who is invisible.

HEBREWS 11:24–25, 27

The making of a freedom fighter
Exodus 1—2

In November 1989, the Berlin Wall came down. You'd think it would have taken some dramatic event to overthrow 40 years of communist oppression, wouldn't you? But apparently not. There were of course all sorts of things going on behind the wall in the late 1980s, each of which may have had its part in bringing the final breakthrough, but the catalyst for the unstoppable events of 9 November was something small and rather dull.

In response to growing protests across the country, the communist government of the German Democratic Republic had made a decision at their general assembly to relax travel restrictions to the West. Though the idea had been agreed, no plan or timescale had been decided on, and this proved something of a problem to the party official who had the job of reporting the outcomes of the assembly to a press conference. When asked how soon travel restrictions would be eased, he waffled for a while and then said that wonderful little word *sofort* (which is German for immediately).

Crowds flocked to the crossing points, and the border guards, overwhelmed by the sheer numbers and unable to get any clarification on what else *sofort* might mean except immediately, opened the barriers – barriers which would never again be closed.

Some 400 years after Joseph and his family had settled in Egypt, the descendants of Abraham, now numerous indeed, found themselves locked down under a great weight of oppression. They were utterly powerless, in a nation where the law was whatever the reigning monarch said it was, and the reigning monarch in question liked having them subjugated, so there was no hope of freedom in sight. The promised land was no longer the home they were going to return to, just as soon as the famine was over. The promised land was a distant, unreachable fantasy.

The Israelites had devised all kinds of ways to mount resistance in the face of their oppressors – midwives who refused to murder babies, to mention but one – but they still needed that one little explosion which would shatter the prison of their slavery once and for all. God's solution was to throw in a firecracker called Moses.

At first glance, Moses didn't look quite right for the part of freedom fighter. He was one of the lucky few Israelites who sidestepped slavery altogether, becoming the adopted grandchild of Pharaoh. Though he must have known something of his roots, he had never personally lived under the tyranny his birth family lived under. How easy it would have been for him to coast through life, enjoying the privileges of status and wealth.

But then, one day, he went out (Exodus 2:11). Who knows why he went out? Perhaps he was bored or wanted to go for a walk or curious to see what the Israelite slave camps were like. Whatever the reason, it proved a life-changing outing in so many ways. By the end of the day, he had become so incensed at the injustice meted out to his own people that he had murdered a man.

Sometimes faith is deciding you're going to do something because God has given you an uplifting, inspiring new dream, and sometimes it's deciding you're going to do something because God has just shown you the messy, depressing reality of gross injustice. Whether it's the beautiful or the ugly that causes you to leap off the end of your own possible into God's impossible, it's still faith and you're still a hero. I once heard somebody say, 'I don't really have a dream. I just think it's outrageous that people have to sleep rough on the streets of our town.'

Do you need to go out? Are you in danger of getting too comfortable in the life God has given you? Is there so much to do that you simply don't have time to look beyond the circle of your own responsibilities? Is it time to carve holes in your busyness so you can see how others are living?

The first reason the writer to the Hebrews gives for Moses being a hero is that he gave up his comfortable life and let God make him an uncomfortable, outraged young man. Is God stirring outrage in you about something? It can be an awkward feeling, can't it? And our tendency is sometimes to try to dampen it for fear of being seen as overdramatic. But it was Moses' outrage that spurred him to action, time and time again.

There is, however, a warning in Moses' story. A couple of verses after he had set out on his life-changing walk, we find him trying to solve the problems of injustice single-handed, by murdering one of the Egyptian slave drivers. The ill-conceived action did nothing to endear him to the people he was trying to free, and he ended up having to flee for his life from his own grandfather.

When outrage is stirred up in you, it's important to learn how to manage it. When God opens your eyes to something terrible, the emotions you feel are crucial – they're part of the fire that will eventually spur you to action – but they're also unreliable advisers. Your emotions may tell you to do things that your brain, in a less outraged condition, would never even consider. When I read this story of Moses' early years, I often wonder if he would have led the Israelites to freedom in the promised land decades earlier if only he hadn't acted on his rage and killed the Egyptian. That impulsive outburst delayed matters by about 40 years.

Moses may have been chastened by his mistake, but he wasn't changed by it. Pan forward a while and we find him rescuing seven women who've been set upon by thuggish shepherds. Moses was a justice champion to the core of his being. Wherever he went, he couldn't help but get involved. This time, though, instead of landing him with a death threat over his head, it landed him with a wife.

Have you let your own mistakes or the mistakes of others dull your passion for justice-seeking? If so, today's the day to fire it up again.

At its root, the quest for justice is a cry from the heart. It will eventually turn into action of some kind, but we do well not to skip the crying part. Exodus 2 ends with Moses stuck miles from home, tending sheep and unable to help his enslaved people. But it also ends with the remarkable reassurance that:

> The Israelites groaned in their slavery and cried out, and their cry for help because of their slavery went up to God. God heard their groaning and he remembered his covenant with Abraham, with Isaac and with Jacob.
> EXODUS 2:23–24

The ingredient which starts the cogs of justice turning is not a hasty act to fix things; it's the cry to God for rescue. Years before that communist official had his awkward press conference, a church in Leipzig had begun hosting prayer vigils every week. The authorities let them happen, because they couldn't imagine how a bunch of people holding candles could be dangerous, but those meetings were the heart cry – the groan which went up to God. And the rest truly is history.

Praying it

Sometimes it helps to get physical in prayer, especially when you're articulating outrage or despair at a terrible situation. And getting physical in prayer is far better than doing something rash or inappropriate.

Activity
Think of a situation that outrages you. Find something you can smash, like an old plate or a tile. Then find a hammer. In a safe place and with proper precautions, smash up your object with the hammer, as a prayerful expression of how much you want God to break the evil of that situation and how desperately you long for him to bring rescue.

Talking it

- Have you ever let yourself get outraged by something? How did it feel? Did you end up acting in some way to change the situation?
- It's all too easy to get stuck in complacency when our lives are comfortable and sheltered. How can we make sure we're keeping our eyes open to injustice?
- Do you have anyone in your church who's involved in fighting for justice? What could you do to ensure they get regular prayer support?

Living it

Fighting together
It's generally better to fight for justice alongside others, rather than on your own. If there's an issue you feel strongly about, why not look for others who share your concern, then get together to talk about

how you might go forward. Remember, though, the cry to God in prayer is always the first step, so make prayer a non-negotiable part of anything you do.

Modern-day slavery

Slavery is as real now as it was in Moses' day. Some 27 million people are estimated to be living as slaves today, whether in the sex industry, in forced labour or domestic servitude. Why not do some research on how to spot modern-day slavery and human trafficking in your local community. You might even want to form a small group to help combat this age-old evil.

Robust conversations
Exodus 3:1–10; 4:1–17; 33:12—34:8

My grandmother was Italian, so we spent many holidays in Italy when I was young. I loved most things about that fair land, especially the food, but there was one aspect of Italian culture which I disliked immensely. You see, Italians don't tend to talk to each other, they shout at each other. I once passed two women in the street who seemed to be tearing strips off one another, but when I asked my mum what they were arguing about, it turned out they'd just been discussing the weather. No matter how much I told myself that the aggressive conversational tone was just the Italian way, it never failed to make me a little anxious.

Reading Moses' story is a lot like listening to an Italian conversation. It is shot through with passion and emotion, and no small amount of anger. At various moments in his story, Moses got angry with Pharaoh, with his own people, and even with God. The Israelites got angry with God and with Moses. And God, for his part, got angry with Pharaoh, with the Israelites and with Moses. That's a lot of anger.

Injustice tends to breed anger. Liberation is a wonderful end, but the process of getting there can be a messy one. If you hail from a culture where conversation is less expressive than it is for Italians, you may share my discomfort at some of Moses' conversations with God. Right at the beginning, in that burning bush encounter, Moses started his first argument with God. The suggestion that he should become God's emissary seemed to cause him so much anxiety that he pretty much told God he was wrong. Unsurprisingly, that made God angry.

And this is where Moses' culture and mine diverge even more. In my brand of reserved, non-confrontational conversation, anger is a thing to be avoided at all costs. It's a volatile, dangerous commodity to be kept for private consumption only. If it does ever surface during an exchange with another person, it should be tidied away beneath a rigidly calm voice and a smattering of words like 'unfortunate'. If the unthinkable happens and anger explodes, the best course of action is to walk away, accepting that that relationship is probably irreparably damaged. It comes as something of a surprise to me then that, having burned with anger against Moses, God just carried on talking to him. The anger was real, and I'm sure Moses felt it, but it didn't stop their communication.

Of course, we have no idea what it was really like to be Moses. All we have are some ancient stories. Yet the Exodus storyteller seems keen for us to realise how turbulent Moses' journey with God was. By comparison, God's exchanges with Abraham, Isaac, Jacob and Joseph seem measured and civilised, whereas Moses' encounters with God look like the roller coaster of a wild romance. There were arguments and stand-offs, but there were also moments of intimacy like nothing we've seen in the scriptures up to that point. Given Moses' contrary attitude, God would have been justified in withdrawing from him, but instead he was allowed closer to God's glory than almost anyone else in the Old Testament.

Fighting for justice is likely to get messy. If you hope to keep your relationship with God polite and rational, then steer clear of becoming a freedom fighter. But if life has planted in you an urgency to fight for change, then be reassured that the one who walks beside you is thrilled to ride the rapids with you. He is not afraid of the mess, and he is not offended by your outbursts. There may be what a vicar of mine used to call 'robust conversations', but there may also be brushes with glory.

Anger is a bit like physical pain. It's an involuntary reaction within us which tells us something is wrong. As such, it's a good and vital part of being human. But we have probably all experienced moments when anger has been used to hurt others. If not managed well, it can become the energy behind abuse and destruction. If not handled well in our relationship with God, it can end up consuming us, so that we can no longer connect with him.

Some of the angriest people in the exodus story were the Israelites themselves. They often 'grumbled in their tents' (Psalm 106:25). Given that they were wandering in a desert, it's not surprising that they felt the need to complain from time to time, but their natural reaction of anger got nurtured into a gnawing bitterness which cut them off from Moses and from God.

Complaint is a vital skill to learn in prayer, because it helps us to direct our anger appropriately. The Israelites complained *about* God, whereas Moses complained *to* God. The Israelites were probably keeping a humble, compliant facade during their times of prayer, then going away to shred God's name in the privacy of their tents. Moses, by contrast, had no qualms about telling God exactly how he felt. On hearing that God was no longer to accompany them into the promised land, but that he would be sending an angel instead – an offer which most of us would have grabbed with both hands – Moses simply refused to accept it. He dug his heels in and insisted that God go with them. I imagine that stand-off led to some awkwardness, but by the end of the exchange, God was willing to appear to Moses in a way he never appeared to the patriarchs before him (Exodus 34:1–8).

If we can overcome the fear that God will disapprove of our anger, we discover a whole new dimension in our closeness to him. If we stew on our anger and rehearse our grievances to those around us but never to God, then our relationship with him will start to feel distant and fake. If we take our complaints straight to God, letting him absorb the full force of our anger, then our relationship with him will become fuller, richer and deeper.

The final thing to note about our fiery freedom fighter is that his complaints to God were unselfish. The Israelites' grumbling was self-obsessed, whereas Moses' complaining was for the good of his people. At one point, God was so furious with the Israelites that he offered to obliterate them and reform his chosen people through Moses and his descendants, but Moses would have none of it, and he wasted no time in telling God that if that was his game, he might as well destroy him too. Moses' anger was not soothed by flattery or promises of personal gain, because it wasn't rooted in self-preservation; it was rooted in wanting something better for others than he wanted for himself.

One of the best ways to keep your anger 'clean' – to stop it rotting into bitterness – is to keep testing your motives. If your anger is mostly rooted in fear, stress or self-pity, bring it to God, let him have the full force of it, but commit to leaving it behind when you've spoken it out to him. But if your anger is rooted in outrage at a situation which is unjust, then don't be afraid to keep hammering it out in your conversations with God until you see something change. God honoured Moses for his stubborn determination to fight for a better world, and he will honour yours too.

Praying it

The Old Testament is full of outraged people expressing their anger to God in prayer, and one of the metaphors they use most often is that of a client engaging God as their prosecution lawyer, to fight an injustice on their behalf.

Activity

You never need to persuade God to act against injustice – it's at the heart of his nature to do that – but one of the ways to express your anger and outrage in prayer is to pretend you're trying to convince a top barrister to act for you. Think about an injustice which is making you angry, then write a speech about why the cause is so deserving. Read it out loud to God, and deliver it with passion; even pace the floor if that helps. Open the floodgates of your frustrations and longings and let him have the lot.

Talking it

- Have you ever experienced a situation where anger has been destructive? What happened, and what effect did it have on you?
- Do you know someone who is active in ending an injustice of some kind? What inspires you about them?
- How can we help one another to avoid the temptation to 'grumble in our tents'? What can we do to help one another not to turn bitter but to keep our anger clean?

Living it

Oil on troubled waters

The resentful, selfish anger which the Israelites experienced is usually rooted in people feeling insecure. Do you know someone who's feeling that kind of anger at the moment? Is there a small act of kindness you could do which would help them to feel less threatened?

Anger to action

One of the ways to help keep your anger clean and unselfish is to keep turning it into action. Inward-looking anger never wants to act, it just wants to wallow, but outward-looking anger wants to make the world a better place. When you find yourself feeling furious about an injustice, work out something practical you can do to help overturn it.

- - - - - - - - -

8

- - - - - - - - -

Joshua

By faith the walls of Jericho fell, after the army had marched round them for seven days. By faith the prostitute Rahab, because she welcomed the spies, was not killed with those who were disobedient.
HEBREWS 11:30–31

Battle stories
Exodus 17:8–16, Joshua 1:1–11

I used to love maths at school, but always struggled to remember that complicated method for calculating sines, cosines and tangents. Then one day, my maths teacher taught us a little rhyme about some man called Silly Old Harry who caught a herring while trawling off America, and suddenly I could remember it with no problem. I can still remember it now.

Stories are invaluable for helping us to learn and remember. It's handy then that the Bible is so full of them. The only trouble is that some of its stories are considerably less palatable than the tale of Silly Old Harry and his herring. They date from a time when politics was more often done by sword-wielding warriors on horseback than by civilised discussions in committee rooms, and though we know we should read them because they're in the Bible, we tend to keep them at arm's length by thinking of them as nothing more than glimpses into a bygone era.

And then we come across Hebrews 11:30 and we discover that the writer actually wants us to view the sacking of an entire city as an act of heroic faith. Nomadic wanderings, boat-building and famine prevention, those are certainly heroic acts of faith, but wiping out a city? What can that story possibly have to teach anyone, especially those of us who live in the slightly more civilised 21st century? What lasting and memorable truth are we supposed to find there?

Perhaps one of the lasting truths is that God's people regularly need to fight battles. We may never need to fight an evil king or an invading army, but we still face the reality of an intentional force of evil in our world. Jesus talked more about that evil presence, whom he named Satan, than he did about many other things. Jesus took Satan seriously, and so did the early church. They never treated that evil power as something to be ignored or downplayed. They firmly believed that it was hell-bent on thwarting the work of God in the world, and they challenged their people to fight against it (James 4:7; 1 Peter 5:8–9).

If there is a battle to be fought against evil, then perhaps a few battle pictures, such as the Jericho story, might be useful after all – provided we don't act out any replays.

Though he doesn't get a mention in Hebrews 11, the man we need to meet, if we're to learn the Jericho lessons, is Joshua, Moses' aide and war chieftain. Despite his passion to fight for justice, Moses didn't do any fighting. Instead, he became the lawgiver who helped set the foundations for how God's people would live, work and worship. Joshua, on the other hand, was a warrior. A story in Exodus 17 gives us a glimpse of how the two men worked together – a story which has some resonances with spiritual warfare today. As Joshua fought the armies of Amalek – a nation whose name came to symbolise a dark, evil power – Moses sat on the hilltop, hands raised to heaven in prayer. While Moses prayed, the battle went in Joshua's favour; but when he didn't, Amalek started to win ground.

When Moses died, Joshua took his place as leader of the people, and it turned out to be a wise succession plan. God knew that the Israelites would have to fight battles as they took up residence in the land he was sending them to. They needed a leader who was also a warrior. Without Joshua they would have been unable to fight the battles they needed to fight, and they might even have ended up returning to slavery in Egypt.

Much like the Israelites, we can't usually stroll in and take the promised lands God has for us without a fight. At the beginning of his letter to the Ephesians, Paul says that God has 'blessed us in the heavenly realms with every spiritual blessing in Christ' (Ephesians 1:3), but by chapter 6 he is instructing his readers on how to stand their ground against the 'spiritual forces of evil in the heavenly realms' (Ephesians 6:12). It's reassuring to know that there's a whole wealth of blessing for us to inherit, but it's sobering to realise we might need to fight for it.

In the summer of 1944, the Allied forces fought their way through northern France to liberate Paris from Nazi control. France is a big country, so it took a long time for news of the liberation to filter through to every outlying village. For many weeks, people in some parts of rural France continued to live as though they were still ruled by Hitler. In some places, German soldiers continued to behave as though they were in charge, despite the news from Paris, in the hopes that the local residents wouldn't find out that they were now free. Even when Nazi power was overthrown, there was still work to do in applying that liberation throughout the whole country, and giving every individual the courage to stand up and resist the remnants of that evil power.

I hope you spot the deeper truths in my battle story.

We are free. Jesus gave his life on the cross, and God raised him from the grave. That mighty work broke every evil power that could ever touch our lives. Satan is utterly defeated by the King of Kings. Yet not everyone everywhere knows they are free and, if we're honest, not every part of our own hearts knows we're free. There are corners which still feel bound and oppressed. The war has been won, but the victory still needs to be communicated and applied. One day, Satan's power will be wiped from the face of the earth, but until then we fight for every soul to discover that freedom has come.

The first chapter of the book of Joshua is a beautiful recounting of God's inaugural promise to Joshua as he took up leadership of the Israelites. God left him in no doubt that he would give him the land – he repeated that bit four times. Joshua went to battle at Jericho fully knowing that God intended to grant the people victory. For Joshua, faith was fighting a battle he knew he had to fight, but doing so from a place of security and confidence, because he knew that the God who walked beside him was also the general who rode ahead of him against the enemy.

Before we go further, let's stop and ponder that remarkable truth: there are battles to fight in our lives, because the enemy of our souls is out to steal, kill and destroy (John 10:10), but we fight those battles in the full knowledge that we will receive the inheritance God has for us. God has immensely good things in store for you, all rolled up in the wrapping of his eternal, unshakeable love, and there is absolutely nothing that can separate you from that love-wrapped gift, no matter how vehemently the powers of darkness may oppose you and your walk with him.

Praying it

The apostle Paul had a peaceful confidence that was a lot like Joshua's. He knew the reality of the battle, but he also knew the certainty of God's victory. That's a certainty we need to remind ourselves of regularly.

Activity

Read Romans 8:38–39, where Paul lists all the things that will never separate him from God's love. Rewrite the verses with your own list of things that threaten to overwhelm you at times, and then read it aloud as a reminder that none of those things is stronger than the victory Jesus won for you on the cross.

Talking it

- Is there a story (from the Bible or otherwise) that has taught you something important and that has stayed with you over the years?
- Are there any Bible stories you find it particularly uncomfortable to read? If so, why?
- It's easy to go to extremes when we think about spiritual warfare, either giving Satan too much credit for things that go wrong, or minimising him and pretending he doesn't exist. How can we help each other to maintain a balanced view of who Satan is?

Living it

Follow Jesus' example

Search your Bible for all the occasions when Jesus talked about Satan. What truths do you learn from what Jesus said about him, and how can you follow Jesus' example in dealing with that intentional, intelligent force of evil?

Slavery unmasked

We get so used to being bound by things that we stop noticing we're not completely free, even though we know Jesus has won freedom for us. As you go about life today, try to stop and notice those areas where you're not yet free – where fear, selfishness or addiction still have you bound. Each time you notice it, give thanks that the battle won't last forever.

Battle strategies
Joshua 5:13–15; 6:1–21; 7:1–26; 10:1–15

Operation Overlord was the Allied offensive which ended in the liberation of Paris, shortly before the end of World War II, and it was essentially a masterpiece of subterfuge. Secret plans were made to land troops on the Normandy coast, but in order to stop the Germans from discovering the strategy, a fake plan was also invented, known as Operation Fortitude. It involved setting up two fake invasion plans, one in Kent and one in Scotland, so that the German High Command would expect attacks to come through Calais and Norway.

The fake plans were almost as ingenious as the real one, involving misleading wireless communications, dummy military vehicles and even a whole fake American regiment. The strategy worked – the Germans believed the fake intelligence and so didn't have enough troops in place to counter the real invasion from the Normandy beaches.

If you're going to fight a battle, it's important to know what kind of battle it is and what strategy will work best. Joshua, Israel's warrior leader, had the responsibility of leading the people to take the land God had sent them to; that meant displacing the local tribes, and that, in turn, meant battles. No two battles were the same, because God was in charge of strategy. The stories of the Israelites routing other peoples to take possession of their land may not make comfortable reading, but Joshua's story does have some helpful tips for us on how to do battle.

First, Joshua had to learn who was in charge. As the people sat encamped in front of Jericho, he had a humbling encounter with God which fundamentally readjusted his attitude. Being a warrior himself, when Joshua met another warrior his first goal was to find out which army he was from; only then could he know if he was in danger. The first thing Joshua learned was that God is not on anyone's side (Joshua 5:13–15). Even in battle, God doesn't come to endorse one side or the other. He comes to do what he wants to do, and the appropriate response to his coming is simply to bow – to surrender our petty little crusades, and to let him take charge.

Do you need to lay down a crusade today? Is there a battle you've been fighting because you're hurt or you feel wronged, and you're trying to persuade God to take up arms on your side? The captain of the Lord's army isn't a mercenary; he is your commander-in-chief. Is he perhaps commanding you to let him decide which battles need to be fought in your life?

The second strategy Joshua had to learn was the one I like to call 'ridiculous obedience' (Joshua 6:1–21). Jericho was an obstacle in the way of the Israelites' path into the promised land, and they couldn't get past it without attacking it. Joshua was a seasoned warrior, and he'd already started working out how they were going to take the city. He had sent spies into it, and he had probably lost hours of sleep doing the logistics. In the end, though, God gave him a strict set of battle orders, and I get the feeling that, had he strayed from them by one tiny degree, they might not have got the victory. Given Joshua's battle experience, it must have taken tremendous faith to do nothing but walk around a wall 13 times, and then shout at it. But he did it, and it worked.

Do you find yourself facing a battle for which you know God has given you a plan, but it just seems ridiculous? If so, stick with it. You may well be about to see a huge obstacle moved out of the way.

Joshua must have been elated by the Jericho victory, but he had a hard lesson to come. I once heard a story about students who were learning to preach under the tutelage of Charles Spurgeon. One of them stood up to deliver a blistering sermon on the armour of God in Ephesians 6, bringing it to a climax with the question: 'Satan, where are you now?' Spurgeon's voice replied from the church balcony: 'Inside the armour!'

Ai looked like an easy target, and Joshua probably concluded that he didn't need to bother God for another creative battle strategy, so he did what he knew to do. He sent spies, he sized up the situation and he dispatched men to take the town, but they failed (Joshua 7:1–5). The Ai defeat was as impossible as the Jericho victory had been.

When Joshua petitioned God, he discovered that there was sin in the camp (Joshua 7:6–13). The rule was that no plunder was to be taken from Jericho, but Achan had kept some of the spoils for himself. God's word through Joshua was stern:

> 'There are devoted things among you, Israel. You cannot stand against your enemies until you remove them.'
> JOSHUA 7:13

We may not be hoarding a 50-shekel gold bar as Achan was, but there are certainly times when our own choices make us unable to withstand enemy attack. I've known times in my own life when I've been nursing a grievance about someone else being treated better than me, someone being preferred over me, and despite God challenging me to let go of my pride, I've chosen to keep hold of it. In those moments, waves of accusation have rolled in – sudden thoughts about how worthless I am. I know exactly where those waves come from, because our enemy is known as 'the accuser' (Revelation 12:10) and 'a liar' (John 8:44). But because I have been nurturing my pride and resentment, I have no strength to resist those accusing thoughts. Instead, I capitulate and start to agree with my accuser, until God's Spirit rescues me with a timely reminder of how loved and liberated I am.

It's worth noting that the process for showing up Achan's sin was done at God's leading, and was very specific. There was no anger-fuelled witch-hunt, just a precise orderly sorting through by God's Spirit. We need to bear that in mind for ourselves. God doesn't ask us to go on some kind of internal witch-hunt to see if we can find any rogue thoughts or actions. He simply asks us to let his Spirit shine light where it needs to be shone, so that we can repent and move forward (1 John 1:5–9).

Sometime after the more successful attack on Ai, the Israelites were called upon to help the Gibeonites fight a ferocious battle against an invading enemy force (Joshua 10:1–15). Joshua led the army out, in answer to the call, and the battle was won by another spectacular God-intervention. For as long as they needed daylight, they had daylight. The sun simply failed to go down. No mighty walls toppled this time; God just made sure they had enough time and strength to win the victory.

I find this one of the most comforting stories in scripture. How often do we wonder if we'll have the strength to see a battle through? Perhaps there's something for which you've been praying for years or there's a particularly painful situation going on for you at the moment, and you wonder how you're going to keep going. The answer is that God will stretch anything that needs stretching, to give you time and energy to see it through. If he has led you into battle, your captain and general will not abandon you. He will lead you to victory.

Praying it

It's helpful to do a battle inventory from time to time.

Activity

Think about one of the battles you're fighting at present, and ask yourself the following questions as you pray:

- Is this a battle God has asked me to fight, or is it a crusade of my own?
- Am I fit to fight, or am I holding on to a sin or wrong attitude that might make me unable to stand up to the enemy of my soul?
- Has God given me a strategy I need to obey?
- What resources do I need from God, to see this battle through?

Talking it

- Do any of Joshua's battle experiences remind you of battles you've fought in the past?
- What can we do to help make sure we're only fighting the battles God wants us to fight, rather than the crusades stirred up by our own injured egos?
- Battles are corporate as well as personal. Which battle is your church fighting at the moment? Are there causes you're standing for or things in your local community you're trying to change?

Living it

Fighting right

Our battle is never against 'flesh and blood' (Ephesians 6:12). We are never to fight people, only the powers of darkness which we see in operation in our world. We oppose those powers with prayer and action, all the while loving the people who get caught in their grip. As you wage war on darkness, be sure to check that you are opposing the power but loving the person. After all, it's often the love that breaks the power over them.

Hand-holding

Exodus 17 tells the story of Moses raising his hands in prayer while Joshua fought the battle. Are you praying for someone who's fighting a battle at the moment, and are your hands getting tired from the work? Why not ask a couple of friends to support you in prayer, just as Aaron and Hur supported Moses. You don't have to tell them any details; just ask them to pray for you as you pray for the person who's battling.

9

Gideon and Samson

And what more shall I say? I do not have time to tell about Gideon, Barak, Samson and Jephthah...

HEBREWS 11:32

The economy of the least
Judges 6:1–24; 7:1–23

'Pardon me, my lord,' Gideon replied, 'but how can I save Israel? My clan is the weakest in Manasseh, and I am the least in my family.'

JUDGES 6:15

I recently heard a young musician being interviewed on the radio. She was about ten years old and had already composed some excellent orchestral music. The interviewer asked her how she felt about the fact that some people were comparing her to Mozart. I assume the interviewer expected the girl to brush off the comparison with a little shrug of embarrassment and some mumbled words about how she couldn't possibly consider herself in the same league as such a great composer. Instead, the girl simply said, 'Well, I don't want to be Mozart. I want to be me.'

I laughed out loud at such a bold and beautiful answer. Children tend to believe in themselves absolutely, don't they? They're not afraid to tell you when they think they've done something well. How is it then that we reach adulthood beset by insecurities and so unable to believe in ourselves?

Amalek was back, only this time they had brought two other ruthless tribes with them. What's more, Joshua the warrior was a distant memory, and Gideon, God's man for the hour, was suffering a serious bout of adult insecurity. Perhaps he'd played at pretend Amalekite-slaying when he was little, but now that he was a grown-up, the reality of having a powerful enemy had cowed him into hiding. The Israelites were in a truly desperate situation. Having established themselves in the land God had sent them to, they had gone back to being oppressed fugitives. If it had taken a Moses and a Joshua to get them out of Egypt, what would it take to get them out of this terrible occupation?

Gideon was understandably daunted at being told he was the man for this particular deliverance. He wasn't a Pharaoh's son like Moses, and he hadn't had years of battle experience like Joshua. He had no skills, except perhaps the threshing of wheat in small spaces. Why on earth did God choose him? Surely someone somewhere had been planning some kind of counter-strategy to overthrow the evil invaders. Why not start with them?

It is a strange feature of God's economy that he often chooses to use people who, on the face of it, look like they stand no chance of succeeding — a desert-dwelling farmer to build a boat; an infertile couple to start a lineage. He delights in confounding our sense of what is possible. He is always more interested in the least than the greatest, so he found himself a man with no status, no reputable family name and no aspirations whatsoever, and then he named him Mighty Warrior. At that moment, it mattered not one iota how much like a warrior Gideon felt. When Creator God speaks a name over you, you will find you have all you need to live up to it.

That being said, there is an important phrase in God's conversation with Gideon which we do well to note: 'Go in the strength you have…' (Judges 6:14). Driving out such a powerful invading force was far beyond the limits of Gideon's capability, but God didn't ask him to swap identities with a superhero or a warlord. He asked him to invest the strength he had. His leap of faith was not to become Joshua or Moses, it was to become Gideon. Then God would take the tiny strength he had and multiply it, till he had all the strength he needed. That is heartening indeed, if you're feeling the need for superhero qualities to cope with life at the moment.

Imagine how encouraged Gideon must have felt when he'd managed to amass an army of 32,000 fighters. Perhaps he finally started believing that deliverance might be possible after all. But God's economy hadn't changed overnight. God was still more interested in the least than the most, and he certainly didn't want the army to take the credit for a work he himself was planning to do, so he started whittling away at it by a variety of means, not least a strange episode of river-drinking.

There's been much speculation on why the cupped-handed drinkers were chosen over the lappers. To my mind, the only reason God chose the cupped-handed ones was because they were the smaller group. Had the lappers been the smaller group, he'd have chosen them. God was all about diminishing Gideon's human resources, so that he could demonstrate his power to work through the least of the least.

How many times have you thought you could just about manage something, only for life to strip away the few resources you had left? One of my more common rants to God revolves around how I'm going to survive my busy day when I haven't had enough sleep. How does he expect me to cope? Why didn't he help me sleep? You get the drift. It's at moments like those that God gently reminds me that he works to a different economy to mine. In mine, strength and ability are all-important; I need to feel I am capable of achieving. In his, trust and dependence are all-important; he has more freedom to work his wonders when I need him and lean on him.

The 300 remaining soldiers set out to an utterly impossible battle, presumably feeling as wobbly about it as Gideon was. But Gideon was catching on fast. When it came to revealing his battle plan, it turned out to be perhaps the least impressive in human history. At a given moment, the 300 men would shout, smash pots (suddenly revealing hidden torches) and blow trumpets. Again, much has been written about how this strategy might indeed have driven the enemy to massacre one another in sheer terror, but I find it hard to believe. I find it easier to believe that God wanted to show Israel again that their God was God of all gods. He wanted to bring absolute victory through the least ideal set of circumstances, to show them that no captivity would ever be so dark that he couldn't rescue them.

There's a lovely little in-joke between God and Gideon in this story. When Gideon accepted the challenge to become God's deliverer for the hour, he wanted to give an offering, so he made a meal which included a huge loaf of bread. We know the loaf was huge because we're told how much flour he used, but we're never told why he made it that way. The angel of the Lord (widely believed to be God the Son before his incarnation) didn't eat the food but instead set it on fire, giving Gideon the time-honoured assurance that his offering had been accepted and that the very presence of God was now right there with him.

On the dawn of the day of battle, Gideon was in need of some courage, so he went snooping around the Midianite camp, where he overheard one soldier telling another soldier about a strange dream he'd had – a dream all about a huge loaf of bread. Gideon must have been reminded of his own mega-loaf, and of that day when the Almighty God had pledged to be with him every step of the way.

You may feel like the least of the least, and your resources may be at zero, but God himself is with you by his Spirit, and he can do remarkable things through the least and the littlest.

Praying it

Gideon's story is full of everyday things, like meat, bread, water, pottery and torches. God could have equipped him with impressive weaponry, but he didn't. Perhaps God is longing for us to learn that 'ordinary' is enough, and that the everyday is exactly where he wants to do miracles.

Activity
Instead of stopping to pray, why not spend your prayer time doing some everyday activities: bake bread, wash the car or clean the house. As you pick up ordinary, unremarkable objects, reflect on the truth that God wants to use you in all your ordinariness.

Talking it

- Have you ever been in a situation where you believed you were too ordinary or unimportant for God to use you?
- Have you ever been in a situation where God has used the most unlikely person or method to get a job done?
- Does your church ever fall into the trap of being so strong and well-organised that you forget how to rely on God? What could you do to stop being so independent?

Living it

Recognising self-reliance
We all have things we rely on to make life that little bit easier – habits, preferences or coping mechanisms which make us feel stronger and more secure. Those things aren't necessarily wrong, but they can stop us relying so much on God. As you go through your day, notice those little things, thank God for them, and remind yourself to lean more heavily on him than you do on them.

Champion the least

Our society does not run according to God's economy of the least. Power, wealth and strength are prized above all things, and those who have the least to offer are often overlooked. How can you speak up for those who are considered the least in your community?

The economy of the weakest

Judges 13:1–5; 13:24–25; 14:1–9; 16:1–31

> **Samson said, 'Let me die with the Philistines!' Then he pushed with all his might, and down came the temple on the rulers and all the people in it. Thus he killed many more when he died than while he lived.**
>
> JUDGES 16:30

During my time with Operation Mobilisation in France (scene of the fainting on the Mormon lady's doorstep), the team I was part of began to run a cafe-bar each Friday night in the church building where we were based. For me, those were the most excruciatingly awkward times of the week – even more awkward than selling Bibles door-to-door – because they were the times when I felt most incapable of making any kind of contribution. The idea was that we would all wander around chatting to members of the public who came in to get a drink, but a room full of chairs and tables is never an easy place for a blind person to navigate, even when there isn't loud music playing in the background. So I would turn up every Friday, sit there with my lukewarm cup of tea and feel thoroughly useless.

Looking back now, I realise that it was in those cafe-bars that I learned to pray. After all, it was the only thing I could do. My friends would come and tell me who was in the room, and I would pray for each person, while the rest of the team got on with the 'real work'. I can't say I embraced this nascent ministry with any enthusiasm – to me it felt like a severe case of 'poor, sad blind girl who can't do anything except pray' – but a couple of decades later, this 'poor, sad blind girl' has made prayer her life's work, and she loves every minute of it.

Sometimes we only really come into our God-strength when we are at our weakest and most helpless.

Having been inspired by Gideon's story, we now come to Samson's, and it has a different flavour altogether. He lived a life rich in rebellion, aggression, bullying and womanising, and it's hard to find even a righteous moment, let alone a great act of faith to celebrate. Yet he merits a mention among the heroes, so we should take a closer look.

Samson was the polar opposite to Gideon. Samson knew he was special and set-apart from his earliest years. He didn't seem to suffer much in the way of adult insecurity. He was confident, charming (in a rugged sort of way) and physically strong. Far from needing to be persuaded to become Israel's deliverer, he took up the job with gusto, getting into scraps with the Philistines (the new enemy on the scene) at every available opportunity. He could tear a lion apart with his bare hands, and he could do mortal damage with a donkey's jawbone. Surely this was exactly the kind of superhero God needed to lead his people and to overthrow their enemies.

One of the most difficult things to understand about Samson's story is that God's power seems to have come to his aid in completely ungodly situations. As a Nazirite, he was subject to an even stricter version of the law than the rest of the Israelites, but he flouted his vows over and over again. He ate from a dead carcass, for instance, which was several violations all in one! He seemed to have scant regard for the lifestyle God had called him to, and yet God's Spirit stayed with him. How is that right or fair?

Grace is a fiendishly tricky business when you're a fair-minded soul. We tend to prefer the notion of karma – life having rules which ensure that the right people get rewarded for the right things – but as we saw in Jacob's story, grace operates on a different system entirely. Grace says that only God can judge the heart of a person, so only he gets to decide who deserves what. Grace is no stranger to giving undeserved gifts to undeserving people. God's grace had the final word on Samson, and it blessed him with supernatural strength, even when he used it to do unrighteous things.

It's easy to frown over Samson, but let's take a moment to examine ourselves. How often do we use a gift or skill that God has given us to achieve something that we know he wouldn't approve of? Some of us have the gift of a sharp wit but use it to belittle others. Some of us are gifted in caring for others but extend ourselves so much that we have little time or space to build relationships with our nearest and dearest. God doesn't withdraw those gifts just because we misuse them. They are the grace-endowments of our creator, and they are ours for life. But we do well to try to use them rightly, because they are far more effective when we do.

Samson's scraps with the Philistines did little to bring Israel much in the way of peace. Note that, despite his physical strength, he never achieved a victory anywhere near as significant as Gideon's. In the end he was captured by the Philistines – ensnared by his lust for beautiful women. Once his hair had been cut, his supernatural strength left him. Why did it happen then? The command not to use a razor on his head was one of many commands given to him as part of the Nazirite vow. How come he could break so many other rules and suffer no ill effects, yet the moment his hair was gone, his strength was taken too?

The genius of grace is that it knows when to give and when to take away. It knows when our weakness can accomplish more than our strength. I remember sitting in those cafe-bar sessions in France, feeling peeved that God wasn't using the gifts he'd given me. My French was better than most people's in the team, so why was I the one sitting in the corner, unable to engage with anyone in conversation, thanks to the frustrations of being blind? Little did

I know that, in taking away my ability to talk to people, God was making room for a whole new gift to grow in me. In my poor, sad, blind weakness, God was working on a far greater plan. Much as I am proud of my ability to speak French, I am absolutely sure that I have made a greater impact in this world through my prayers than I ever have through my French conversation.

Samson had lost everything. His enemies were partying at his downfall, and the future for Israel looked bleak. He was going to die. And it was then, in his weakest, darkest, blindest moment that he finally prayed. He asked for one more burst of strength, only this time he didn't use it to make himself look impressive. He used it to overthrow Israel's enemy, even though it meant giving his own life. Right at the end of his journey, Samson took a leap of faith which won another season of freedom for his people.

Our God-given strengths are wonderful, but our God-given weakness is even more precious. God's economy values weakness, because that's the place where we look to him for strength. Your weakness may feel like a barrier and a closed door at the moment, but stay with it and try not to despise it. It's highly likely to be the gateway to things you've never even dreamed of.

Praying it

God gives us gifts, but he judges us by what's in our hearts. A gift used out of a desire to bless will always bring blessing, but a gift used out of a desire to better ourselves or diminish others will be far less effective.

Activity
Take an honest look over the past week of your life. Can you think of times when you have used one of your gifts – something you're good at or something you have a talent for – out of a wrong motive? Take some time to repent and ask God's forgiveness, and choose to live differently this week.

Talking it

- Has there been a time when you have seen grace at work – undeserved things happening to undeserving people?
- Has God ever opened a new door for you in life as a result of a time of great weakness?
- How can we make sure our churches are communities where grace has the final word? What might that look like? How do we balance grace and justice?

Living it

Temptation alert

Samson finally lost his strength because he allowed himself to be tempted. Temptations come and go, but we don't have to listen to them or give them airtime in our minds. In what situations are you most likely to be tempted to do something that will dishonour God? How can you avoid those situations?

Acting in weakness

Samson had little strength at the end, but he still put it to use. He didn't ask God to topple the Philistine temple, he asked God to help him topple the temple. Is there an area of life where you feel weak at the moment? Don't give up just because you feel defeated. Think of one tiny act of obedience you could put into practice today. You might be surprised at how effective it turns out to be.

10

David

... about David and Samuel and the prophets, who through faith conquered kingdoms, administered justice, and gained what was promised...

HEBREWS 11:32–33

The art of trusting
1 Samuel 24:1–22; 26:1–12; 2 Samuel 24:1–25

I am frequently tempted to micromanage. My husband and I usually end up having to strike a deal that if I'm going to ask him to do something, I need to let him do it his way rather than popping in every ten minutes to advise him on how he should be doing it. Once you've entrusted a task to someone, it's generally a good idea to let them get on with it.

One of the last people to get a personal mention in Hebrews 11 is David. Though the writer only mentions him in passing, his story is remarkable. While he was still looking after the family sheep – a menial task that would have been given to the youngest and least capable member of the family – the prophet Samuel turned up to anoint him king of Israel. It was the economy of the least yet again confounding the human understanding of greatness. Since the nation had only just got its first king, no one knew what royal succession would be like, but David must have thought he'd got off to a good start, since he quickly became King Saul's personal music therapist, and then single-handedly dispatched Goliath, one of Israel's most terrifying enemies. Unfortunately, David had yet to learn about the strange things that happen to a person who has power and doesn't want to let go of it. For over a decade, Saul resisted him and tried to kill him. On two occasions, he threw a spear at him while he was playing his harp.

David's road to kingship was a harried flight through Israel's wildest terrain, hiding out and trying to avoid assassination, but his years as a shepherd had forged a simple, iron-strong trust in God which he never let go of. On the brink of the battle with Goliath, he summed it up for Saul:

> 'I've been a shepherd, tending sheep for my father. Whenever a lion or bear came and took a lamb from the flock, I'd go after it, knock it down, and rescue the lamb. If it turned on me, I'd grab it by the throat, wring its neck, and kill it. Lion or bear, it made no difference – I killed it. And I'll do the same to this Philistine pig who is taunting the troops of God-Alive. God, who delivered me from the teeth of the lion and the claws of the bear, will deliver me from this Philistine.'
>
> 1 SAMUEL 17:34–37 (*THE MESSAGE*)

As far as David was concerned, God knew best, God was always right and God would always come through for those who put him first. Was it the oversimplistic philosophy of a child? Maybe, but he held on to it throughout his life, and he is known as the greatest earthly king Israel ever had. When Jesus is content to bear the name Son of David, you can be sure David was doing something right.

David believed that when you trust God to work things out, you also have to let him do it his way. Circumstances afforded him at least two opportunities to kill Saul, and his closest advisers thought he should do it. Given Saul's murderous intent towards him, it would have been a legitimate act of self-defence. And after all, he was meant to be king. God had already abandoned Saul and was manifestly with

David instead, so why not use human means to advance God's own ends?

> 'As God lives, either God will strike him, or his time will come and he'll die in bed, or he'll fall in battle, but God forbid that I should lay a finger on God's anointed.'
> 1 SAMUEL 26:10–11 (*THE MESSAGE*)

For David, revenge, self-defence and expediency were not good excuses for doing something. It was certainly costlier and more painful to wait for God's resolution, but it was the right thing to do if he really wanted to uphold his principle of trusting God above all things.

It's not at all unusual for our trust in God to wobble, right in the middle of a faith-leap. Having said yes to the idea of heading for something which is far beyond us, far outside our own limitations, and having committed to trust God as we jump off the end of ourselves, we often experience a sudden sickening vertigo and start to question whether he really will come through for us. It's then that the temptations sneak in: what if I just did this to help things along; wouldn't it help God's cause if I took this little shortcut? If you jumped in obedient faith, trusting God to land you safe in a new place, now is not the time to start trying to make it work without him. Let him finish what he has started.

Once he'd become king, David had a moment of vertigo. The background is tricky to understand, since it seems that God stirred him up to take a course of action that God later regretted (2 Samuel 24:1), but the bare bones of the story are that David got fixated on the results of a census. Censuses were normally taken to see how many fighting men there were in a population, a way of reassuring a ruler that they had enough troops to fight off any enemies. But David had always trusted God to provide for him in battle, and Israel's history was testimony to the fact that numbers meant nothing when it came to God's ability to deliver a victory. Yet David seems to have set too much store by the counting. In *The Message*, Eugene Peterson says that David had started 'replacing God with statistics'.

When you're walking in faith, it pays not to look too closely at the mechanics of how it's all working. The moment you start to count and calculate, you're likely to start feeling distinctly queasy. God can shrink time and multiply money; he can change the fabric of the universe and produce things out of nothing. If you're getting into something on his terms, then you're going to have to get used to things not making much sense, humanly speaking. He will do his working out, but he will not make it fit our equations.

I belong to a prayer community in Canterbury, and we have recently renovated our premises. We were praying about what to do with one of the rooms on our first floor, and felt strongly that we should make it into a high-quality meeting room, for use by groups who needed somewhere to meet but who couldn't afford commercial hire rates. We were looking for some professional-quality boardroom chairs, but we had little money, so I put the word out and within a few weeks had been offered three sets of old church chairs that were surplus to requirements. It would have been easy to accept them as a fantastically cheap solution to our dilemma, but we knew they weren't the right solution, so we turned them down.

It took six months of prayer and waiting before we finally found our set of high-quality, matching boardroom chairs, and they ended up costing us a tiny amount, which even we could afford. God's solution was worth the wait.

If we trust God enough to step out in faith, then we must also trust his economy, his statistics and his way of doing things. We may need to walk past what look like unmissable opportunities to make things happen, but his way will always be the best, most complete and most perfect route to where we're going.

Praying it

David was a musician and a poet. He wrote songs about his trust in God, many of which are now part of the Old Testament.

Activity
If you don't already, why not start using music and poetry in your prayer times. Whether you write your own or read or listen to what others have written, find some rhymes and melodies which help you reaffirm your trust in the God who truly knows what's best for you.

Talking it

- Have you ever felt frustrated by how long God was taking to resolve something for you, and taken a short cut to try to get there quicker? How did it turn out? What happened?
- David's trust lessons began in childhood, while he tended sheep. What do you remember learning about God as a child? Has it stuck with you in adulthood?
- Administration and organisation are good things in church life, but how do we make sure that they don't get in the way of us trusting God?

Living it

Hinge words
Many of the psalms written by and for David have little 'hinge phrases' in the middle. They start out as bleak laments, but suddenly change direction, turning on a single phrase, to become songs of trust and hope. (For example, Psalm 31 has hinge phrase in verses 14 and 15.) Choose a hinge phrase which you can say to yourself in those moments when it is hard to keep trusting.

Teaching trust
David learned to trust God as a child, and that must have been taught to him by an adult. With that undergirding, he became one

of the greatest leaders of all time. Why not make time for someone younger than you, and share with them something about God which inspires you.

The art of being trustworthy
2 Samuel 9:1–12; 11:1–27; 23:13–17

> **After removing Saul, he made David their king. God testified concerning him: 'I have found David son of Jesse, a man after my own heart; he will do everything I want him to do.'**
> ACTS 13:22

I have been part of The Salvation Army all my life. As well as being the part of the church which I call home, it is also the part of the church that most challenges me to keep notching my faith up from reasonable to radical, because its history is packed with stories of ordinary people letting God hijack them for his kingdom purposes. William Booth, Salvation Army founder, didn't set out to form a denomination or start a movement; he set out to preach the good news of Jesus on the streets of London. But as he did that, he started to notice people. He noticed men and women who slept on the streets, girls who were trafficked for sex, families who were starving because the mother or father was drinking the wages away every week – people who were cared for less than the horses which drew the London hackney cabs. And because of those people, Booth and The Salvation Army started doing things they'd never planned to do: homeless shelters, soup kitchens, rehabilitation hostels, safe houses for former sex workers, children's homes, employment exchanges and training centres, to name but a few.

I often find myself wondering where this global movement, now active in almost 150 nations of the world, would be by now if Booth hadn't let himself get distracted. If he had just preached the gospel and planted congregations of believers – a worthy faith-goal indeed – would as many lives have been touched and transformed? We'll never know, because this passionate evangelist chose to let the needs of desperate people reroute him into a fuller expression of what the kingdom of God looks like.

If you read the story of King David, one of the things you notice is that he took his relationships with people seriously. When you're on your way to kingship, there are many who'd suggest you should be ruthless towards those around you, not letting yourself be distracted or derailed by their needs. But David didn't live that way. Maybe it was because he had always found God to be absolutely trustworthy, and so he wanted to model that same integrity. If simple trust was at the heart of his relationship with God, then he wanted it to be at the heart of people's relationships with him as king.

David was intensely loyal. When he made a commitment to someone, he didn't forget it. In his young adulthood, he struck up a firm, deep friendship with Saul's son Jonathan, and though Jonathan died when David was about 30 years old, David maintained the vows and commitments of that friendship for the rest of his life. He had promised Jonathan that, should anything happen to him or his father, he would make sure their family was cared for – a promise he also made to Saul. So when he had established his palace in Jerusalem, he deliberately set out to look for any relatives of Saul and Jonathan who were still alive. He found just one man, Mephibosheth, who was disabled. Disability was considered a curse in those days, and disabled people were deemed unsavoury to have around, particularly in the presence of a king, but David invited Mephibosheth to eat at his own table every day. On the one hand, that was a startling level of loyalty – no one would have blamed him for 'forgetting' his vow to Jonathan, now that the family had been more or less wiped out. On the other hand, it was astonishingly countercultural – choosing to honour someone who had no honour or status in society at all.

Plans are important, but people matter more. Having a dream or a faith-goal is a wonderful thing, but if we become so focused on it that people get trampled along the way, then we're not living the values of Jesus' kingdom. No matter what we are called to, and no matter what dream we pursue, none of us is exempt from the simple mandate of Jesus to communicate hope to the poor, the imprisoned, the blind and the broken-hearted. If you like, it's God inviting us to join him in practising the economy of the least. Take time out to do that, and God will keep your dream safe till you can get back to it.

David wasn't just loyal; he also had an extravagant way of valuing people. In one of the stranger stories of his life, we read of the time when he blurted out an offhand desire for a drink of Bethlehem water, and his three mighty men (all of whom loved a chance to prove themselves) promptly went and stormed the Philistine garrison at Bethlehem to get him some. When they brought it back, he refused to drink it, because it had come to him at the risk of their lives, and their lives were precious to him. Instead he poured it out on the ground as an offering to God. I imagine they may have felt an odd mix of frustration and appreciation at such a bizarre expression of love.

Perhaps that's why the story of Bathsheba and Uriah seems so astonishingly cruel by contrast. This man of integrity, who welcomed a social outcast to his table and who valued his men so highly that he poured out their gift to him as an offering to God, slept with another man's wife just because he wanted to and then had her husband killed just because he could. What's more, that husband was part of that elite force he valued so much – the same force he'd been with when his mighty men brought him the water. In that moment of selfish desire, he started disposing of people instead of valuing them.

Faith may indeed involve a focused, determined push to reach a particular promised land, but the one who walks beside us is the one who stopped to heal blind men, touch lepers, hug children and hear the stories of the overlooked. If we find ourselves next to people for whom he would have stopped, then he will expect us to stop for them too.

But won't we get overwhelmed if we try to help everyone? Yes, of course. It isn't your job to solve the problems of everyone you meet. Had William and Catherine Booth never picked up any fellow soldiers along the way, The Salvation Army would have helped few people indeed. If David hadn't had the resources of a kingly court at his disposal, he would have been far less able to bless and support Mephibosheth. It isn't you or me who make sure people are valued and cared for; it's us together. And if we're going to do that, it will be by God's strength alone.

Paul's description of David as a man after God's heart is beautiful (Acts 13:22). If this book were about the human way to be a hero, I'd be suggesting you storm your way to success, doing your best to avoid letting people drag you down – unless of course you can make yourself look a bit more heroic by helping them. But this is a book about faith heroes, and faith heroes are men and women after God's heart.

God's heart is a busy place. It is full of promised lands and far-away impossible dreams, but it is also full of people who matter. He keeps both emphases in perfect balance. Seek to be a person after his heart, and so will you.

Praying it

If we look at everyone in need around us, we get overwhelmed. If we look at Jesus, he steers our gaze towards those he wants us to notice.

Activity

Spend time picturing Jesus. You might like to do that in your mind's eye or you might prefer to look up an artwork depicting him. As you gaze at his face, ask him to bring to mind a person who he wants you to help today. Once you've identified who it is, pray for them and ask Jesus what he'd like you to do for them.

Talking it

- Have you ever been shown real value by another person? What did they do or say, and why did it touch you so deeply?
- How do you know when it's right for you to help someone and when it's not?
- How can we better work together as churches, so that we can help more people out of poverty and captivity?

Living it

Welcome interruptions

Our lives are often so full and busy that we have no time to stop and talk to people, let alone help them in practical ways. What could you cancel this week, so that you can give that time to someone else? You may know someone who needs some practical help, or you may just wish to walk around the area where you live and see who God steers you to talk to.

Living loyalty

Is there a friendship you know you've neglected of late? Perhaps the busyness of life has got in the way or perhaps a misunderstanding has created distance between you. If you sense God's prompting, why not make contact with that person today and arrange to meet up?

11

Daniel

... who shut the mouths of lions, quenched the fury of the flames, and escaped the edge of the sword; whose weakness was turned to strength; and who became powerful in battle and routed foreign armies.

HEBREWS 11:33-34

Rhythms of prayer
Daniel 6:1-28

When Daniel learned that the decree had been signed and posted, he continued to pray just as he had always done. His house had windows in the upstairs that opened toward Jerusalem. Three times a day he knelt there in prayer, thanking and praising his God.

DANIEL 6:10 (*THE MESSAGE*)

I once went on a tour of John Wesley's house in East London. We started upstairs, looking around his bedroom and his dressing room, which he repurposed as a prayer room, and all of us felt that familiar mix of awe and guilt as we heard how this 18th-century hero of the faith would get up very early in the morning and spend a couple of hours in prayer, before going downstairs to meet the world. We murmured among ourselves about how busy our lives are, with work and family and household chores, and how we obviously need to get our act together and force more space into our days.

The next stop on the tour was John's kitchen, where the tour guide proudly showed us the largest teapot I have ever seen. He told us how John's house was always full of visitors, from dawn till dusk, and how no one in need was ever turned away, and our admiration was ratcheted up by several more degrees. This man must have been a wonder to care for the needy, preach to thousands and still maintain a two-hour-a-day prayer habit. And then the tour guide said the single word which burst our admiration bubble: John Wesley had a housekeeper. Ah well, wouldn't we all get a lot more prayer done if we had a housekeeper? For me, the salutary answer to that question is 'probably not'. I tend to find that the chores of life expand to fill whatever space is available in my life, and prayer easily gets squeezed out, even when I'm not busy.

Daniel was busy. He was vice-regent over a Persian kingdom, which effectively meant he ruled it on behalf of Emperor Darius. He line-managed over 120 other regional governors and he was known to be a wise man, so we can assume his counsel was sought all day every day. Yet he was uncompromising in his attitude towards prayer. No amount of busyness squeezed it out of his schedule.

In our consumerist society, it's easy to think of prayer as a transaction. If I pray enough of the right kind of prayers, then I will get the things I'm asking for. It's what we sometimes call the 'vending machine' approach – I put the right coins in and the right thing pops out. It's a profoundly unhelpful view of prayer for two reasons: first, it produces guilt, because we seldom think we've prayed enough or got it right; and second it produces disappointment, because God isn't a vending machine, and he doesn't behave like one.

Prayer isn't a transaction; it's an interaction. It is the intrinsic connection between us and God. When we don't pray, God is no less real, but he is considerably less connected to us and us to him. His Spirit still lives in us, but without prayer, we're just housemates in the same body, instead of being the close-knit family partnership we're meant to be. The 19th-century writer and theologian Martin

Farquhar Tupper said, 'Prayer is the slender nerve that moves the muscle of omnipotence.'

Imagine that: the omnipotence of God, all his power, all his strength, all his energy and all his life, made available to us through that simple, fragile little thing called prayer.

In many ways, Daniel may be a better role model for us than someone like John Wesley. The Hebrew tradition was not necessarily to spend hours in prayer in the morning, but to punctuate the day with moments of prayer. There's no doubt that a longer, focused time of prayer is important, but if prayer is to be an ongoing interaction, then we need to learn how to stay connected throughout the day, just as Daniel did. We need to carve spaces in our busyness, to be still in his serenity. We need to develop a rhythm of prayer.

Daniel's prayer rhythm had three hallmarks. First, he withdrew to a different place. He went from his office to his bedroom. There was no particular obligation for him to do this, but perhaps he had the words of King Solomon floating in his mind:

> And when a prayer or plea is made by anyone among your people Israel – being aware of their afflictions and pains, and spreading out their hands towards this temple – then hear from heaven, your dwelling-place.
> 2 CHRONICLES 6:29–30

The temple was long gone, but the act of withdrawing and turning himself towards that place was a vital part of Daniel's prayer connection to God. What could you do to intentionally withdraw from the activity of life, and to turn yourself towards God?

Second, Daniel's most regular prayer was one of thanksgiving and praise. I would have to confess that the times I most manage a rhythm of prayer throughout my day are the times when I most need God's help. It's the need that drives me to my knees (inwardly at least), and suddenly my prayer becomes frequent and fervent. Yet for Daniel the stopping wasn't about asking; it was about acknowledging God for who he is and thanking him for what he had done. I'm sure Daniel did ask for help from heaven, but that wasn't the main reason for his praying.

Are you as committed to stopping to give thanks as you are to stopping to ask for help? It is in giving thanks and praise that we remind our fickle hearts of exactly who it is that walks with us.

Third, Daniel's prayer rhythm was non-negotiable. No matter what happened around him, he didn't let go of it. Even when it could have cost him his life, he refused to let it drift. Why? First and foremost, because God was worth it, and second, I presume, because life in Babylon was simply not doable without it. Babylon was a nation fascinated by the magic arts, and its leaders tended to be those who could wield supernatural power. Daniel would have been surrounded by people using some pretty dark magic. He was deemed one of the most powerful magicians around, so he was put in charge of the others, much to their disgust. Of course, the only power he called on was the power of God, but in the dark haze of a court full of sorcerers, he must have become more and more dependent on that regular, deep, life-giving connection with the source of all goodness and light.

Maybe you're not daily surrounded by people practising dark magic, but you certainly will encounter the shadow of evil from time to time. Whether it's the poisonous pursuit of power, the suffocation of despair, the corruption of greed or the oppression of injustice, you're likely to feel the effects of darkness around you. Prayer keeps you close to the one who is inextinguishable light.

The writer to the Hebrews doesn't mention Daniel by name, but does applaud heroes who 'shut the mouths of lions' (Hebrews 11:33). Daniel didn't set out to be a lion tamer, but something happened in that cave to prevent the lions from mauling him. Something about that strong, deep prayer connection he'd forged with his God over so many years enabled him to take control of the situation. It is one of the greatest mysteries of the Christian faith, but there is no doubt that when we steep ourselves in regular prayer, God is somehow able to work through us and around us more powerfully than when we don't. As we get into the habit of connecting regularly with him, God's omnipotence touches the bruised and broken around us and brings new life.

Praying it

Over the centuries, many monastic orders have developed daily prayer rhythms – regular times when they would stop, down tools and go to the monastery church to pray. They would typically use liturgies – set prayers and readings – to guide their praying through the day.

Activity
There are plenty of excellent daily prayer liturgies online, comprising prayers to be used at different times of the day. Why not print one out and use it every day for a week, to help you develop a new prayer rhythm? (The Northumbria Community is a good place to start, for instance.)

Talking it

- What is it in your life which most gets in the way of prayer? How could you stop it being such an obstacle?
- Daniel didn't hide his prayer rhythm. How would you feel if your colleagues, family or friends saw you 'withdrawing' to pray a couple of times a day?
- Has prayer ever got you into trouble, like it did for Daniel?

Living it

Persecuted family
Persecution didn't end with Daniel, and many Christians today live in places where they are not free to practise their faith publicly. Research what life is like for Christians under persecution today, and when you stop to pray throughout your day, remember them in prayer too.

Gratitude journal
If you're less practised in the art of thanksgiving than the art of asking for help, try keeping a gratitude journal, either in a notebook or on your phone. Stop to write in it several times a day, recording the things God has done for you in the past few hours.

Seasons of prayer
Daniel 9:1–23

> **So listen, God, to this determined prayer of your servant. Have mercy on your ruined Sanctuary. Act out of who you are, not out of what we are.**
>
> DANIEL 9:17 (*THE MESSAGE*)

In May 2016, with Britain's EU Referendum just around the corner, I was involved in leading a prayer day. Politics can be a contentious business, particularly with a single-question referendum at stake, so feelings were running high. What's more, when you gather people for prayer, you have the added complexity that some of them believe God has a strong view on how everyone should vote and that belief can lead to the dangerous conclusion that those who plan to vote the other way must be in disagreement with God. That can make for a pretty divisive prayer meeting!

I don't believe God tells us how to vote – I believe he entrusts that decision to us – but I do have a little sympathy for my praying friends who just want God to download a clear message to tell us all which box to tick. This world is a baffling place. In the end, the prayer day was a positive experience. The complexities of the situation kept us firmly focused on God, and we worked hard to push our own opinions aside so that we could stand together in unity, calling for God's kingdom to come and his will to be done.

Daniel knew about complexity. He was a political leader with two countries on his heart: Babylon, his adopted home, and Israel, his true home. Humanly speaking, Israel had ceased to exist, but Daniel was in touch with a more far-sighted vision. Far beyond the exile, far beyond what looked possible to human eyes, he could see the restoration promised by God through Jeremiah. He knew that someone would need to keep hold of that vision, no matter how impossible it seemed, and pray until it was reality.

Daniel had his regular prayer times throughout the day, but he also set aside whole seasons for prayer. On two occasions in his story, we read of him fasting for prolonged periods of time, and in chapter 9 we find him hunkered down in an intense period of repentance and intercession. A rhythm of short prayer moments throughout our day is vital, but those brief interludes will never be the times when we can go deep with God. For the complex things of life, we need time and space in God's company, uninterrupted and open-hearted.

When do you go in deep? When do you shut out the world and get down to the nitty-gritty with God? You can do it wherever suits you best – Daniel had one of his most powerful encounters on a river bank – but you need to do it somewhere. Life will throw you some knotty problems, and you need to develop the art of untangling them in prayerful conversation with God.

Daniel's prayer in chapter 9 was more wailing than chatting. Decades in Babylon hadn't dulled his desperate desire to see Israel restored, and the passion of his pleading reached God's ears. Things were set in motion to begin the rebuilding. Throughout the Bible, we see God's heart being moved by the yearnings of his beloved. It's another of those mysteries: if God knows what's best and he's going to do it anyway, then why does it matter how ardently we pray? Our emotions are God-given; they're not the inconvenient spillage from an over-sensitive soul. When we pray from the current of our emotions, it is a different prayer to the one we form in the workshop of our reason, and it has a different kind of impact.

My husband and I were sitting in a cafe in London one day, needing to make an important decision about the continuation of our fertility treatment. I had been praying about it for months, but I felt so confused and desperate that day that I could no longer keep it all tidied away in the reasoning part of my mind. Instead, I just cried. I would have preferred not to cry in that busy cafe, but you can't always choose where you're going to do your emotional interceding. Having wept out my prayer, I tried to explain it in coherent words to the wonderful man who has been my intrepid co-adventurer for 20 years now, and suddenly we both knew the right way forward. Why hadn't God made it clear six months earlier? Did he want to see me suffer? No, of course not. He's not cruel. But he certainly seemed to be waiting for that heart-cry to surge up from within me, and when it did the prayer was immediately answered.

Do you need to do some fervent intercession? Is there something you keep mentioning in your daily prayers which you know you need to give more time to? You needn't necessarily wear sackcloth like Daniel did, but it would be well worth setting aside a decent chunk of time (at least an hour), finding a place where you feel safe and where you're not likely to be interrupted, and pouring your heart out to God in prayer. Remember, we all process our emotions differently, so you won't necessarily cry like I did in that cafe. The important thing is that you are expressing the depths of your emotions to God, in whatever way feels most natural for you.

Daniel's prayer was also well-informed. In his quest to hold his homeland in his heart, he had obviously studied the prophetic writings that had been sent to the exiles in Babylon some 70 years earlier. He knew from Jeremiah's prophecies that his people's captivity in Babylon was only meant to last 70 years, and then God would bring them home again. As well as being a heartfelt plea, his prayer was a reminder to God that the promise was due its fulfilment.

When you set your heart and mind to pray, do you know what has been promised to you? The scriptures are full of promises, made originally to people centuries ago but still as fresh and true now as they were the day God spoke them. They are his words, so they don't fade away with time. Brother Andrew, founder of Open Doors, tells a story about Corrie ten Boom, a remarkable Dutch lady who had survived a Nazi concentration camp. He said that when they prayed together, she would stand up, open Bible in hand, and tap the page, saying to God: 'Look! Your word says you will do this, so please do it!'

It sounds a little impertinent, doesn't it? But the angel Gabriel, who came in response to Daniel's page-tapping, didn't call him rude or cheeky; he called him 'greatly beloved' (Daniel 9:23, NKJV). God gave us the gift of the Bible so that we would read it, ingest it and remember it. When we know what it says, and we quote it back to him, he is honoured and delighted.

There's a tiny detail in the Daniel 9 story which harks back to the lions' den story in chapter 6. When God's angel arrived, the sign that Daniel's prayers were being answered, he flew in during the time of the evening sacrifice. That was one of Daniel's regular prayer times. If he hadn't set aside that time to pray – if he'd been too busy to follow his prayer rhythm that day – he might have missed the answer altogether. Prayer is about making time in our day to consciously connect with God, but it is also about being available for him, present and focused, so that he can bring us wisdom, strength and hope – and the answers we've longed for.

Praying it

Daniel's prayer of intercession is a useful model for our own. He started by telling the truth about the desperate situation his people were in, then he told the truth about who God was. Last of all, he prayed one key prayer: 'Act out of who you are, not what we are' (Daniel 9:17, *The Message*).

Activity
Make your own prayer of intercession. Choose a situation you feel deeply about, and tell God the truth of it. He knows already, but the cry of your heart is powerful in prayer. Then use your Bible to declare some of the truths about who God is. When you've done that, ask him to intervene, bringing all his love and goodness to bear on that difficult situation.

Talking it

- What was the most emotional prayer you ever prayed?
- Have you ever been in a situation where you've been praying with a group of people about a complex situation on which you disagree? How did you handle it? What was good about it and what was difficult?
- What are your best tips for getting to know the Bible better?

Living it

Bible disciplines
Have you ever tried reading the Bible in a year? If not, it can be an excellent way to get to know the corners you haven't discovered yet. You can find reading plans on the Internet or by downloading a Bible app to your phone or tablet.

Praying destiny
After Daniel had prayed, the doors opened for the people of Israel to return to their promised land and re-establish their lives there.

Our nations need prayer, too. Why not pick a matter of national importance, and commit to praying into it regularly over the coming months, until you see something change? If you can find people to partner you in your praying, even better.

12

The Shunammite woman

Women received back their dead, raised to life again. There were others who were tortured, refusing to be released so that they might gain an even better resurrection.
HEBREWS 11:35

The gift of reformatting
2 Kings 4:8–17

A few weeks ago, I was walking through a part of London which is currently the subject of much reformatting. Consequently, I never know whether the buildings, pavements and road crossings will be in the same place as they were the last time that I was there. My guide dog seemed to be having trouble finding a particular crossing, so I assumed that it had moved.

A cheery gentleman responded to my general call for help, and I explained where I was trying to go. He didn't know the road or the building I was heading for, but that didn't daunt him. He rallied a large group of passers-by, held a long discussion with each of them about where my destination might be, then planned a convoluted route around several underpasses and a footbridge. Fortunately, a woman in the crowd took pity on me before he could lead me off on the route-march of a lifetime, and pointed out that the crossing I wanted was actually right next to where I was standing. Perhaps the dog just wanted a good laugh.

If you've ever received the kind of help which can best be described as unhelpful, you'll have a lot of sympathy for the last hero we meet in this book. Much like Daniel, the writer of Hebrews doesn't mention her by name, but she is one of the first people I think of when I read verse 35: 'Women received back their dead, raised to life again.'

The Shunammite woman was content with her lot. She was relatively well off and had a nice home and a good husband. Though the couple hadn't been blessed with children, we can assume she'd made her peace with that state of affairs, because she entertained Elisha, the man of God, without once asking him to intercede with God on their behalf for a family – a practice that would have been normal in her day.

But sometimes people are just determined to help you, no matter what you do or say to put them off. Elisha and his servant Gehazi were exactly that kind of determined. They started trying to solve problems she didn't have. Did she need something from the king? Could they put in a good word for her with the military? Was her home secure? If the Shunammite woman had a motto, it would have been 'Everything's all right, thank you', and that's exactly what she told them. But then Gehazi had a brainwave. She hadn't had a child, and surely every woman wanted that, so that must be the best thing they could do for her.

If you've ever had the experience of finding peace in a painful situation, only to have the whole thing stirred up again, you'll know something of how she felt when Elisha spoke the prophecy over her. 'No, my Lord!' she objected. 'Please, man of God, don't mislead your servant!' (2 Kings 4:16). The word 'mislead' has a meaning which falls somewhere between lie and disappoint. What Elisha thought would be a great blessing felt to her more like the worst kind of con. She didn't receive the news with a great burst of joy; she received it with a pang of grief and pain.

We have talked often in this book about how it feels to have a dream, to take a faith-leap towards something you long for. Sometimes though, faith is less about jumping and more about being pushed. The Shunammite woman had found contentment, but God wanted to give her something she wasn't asking for. She had settled her life into a format which worked for her, only for God to turn up and reformat it.

There's great comfort here for those of us who have felt guilty about our inability even to believe things God has said to us (either directly or through others), let alone to embrace them. There is a strand of faith teaching which suggests that if you don't immediately receive, believe and give thanks for the promise, it will flutter away again like a fickle paper bird. God's promises are not flimsy, flighty creations; they're eternal truths. God didn't withdraw the promise of a child, just because the Shunammite woman couldn't even begin to accept it when she first heard it. In fact, we don't know whether she ever came to believe it, until the evidence was incontrovertible.

If you think God might have promised you something, but you're not sure and you're loathe to believe it, just in case you're getting your hopes up, then relax. It's not going anywhere. It's a strong, solid stone, dropped into the pool of your life. There is time for you to get used to it, and for the ripples of confusion and dismay to subside.

The Shunammite woman probably didn't realise it, but she set herself up for having her life reformatted the moment she had a conversation with her husband about an extension. She was obviously a God-fearing woman, and wanted to honour the prophet who came through their town from time to time, so she hit on the idea of building him his own room on her roof. In those days, men like Elisha were considered carriers of God's power, so in welcoming him to stay regularly at her home, she was welcoming the power of God to take up residence. Little did she know that when you welcome in the power of God, you leave yourself wide open to being reformatted.

I have worked for many years with the 24-7 Prayer movement, a worldwide, non-stop prayer meeting which started in Chichester, England, in September 1999. At the heart of 24-7 Prayer's vision is the setting up of 'prayer rooms': spaces which are decked out creatively and then prayed in, night and day for days, weeks, months, even years. Much like the Shunammite woman, when we set aside a space solely for the purpose of welcoming God's presence and power, the results can be somewhat surprising. In preparation for writing this chapter, I did a small survey to see how many of my friends had had unexpected 'reformatting' moments while they were in a prayer room, and the responses were swift, numerous and splendidly varied. Some had heard a call to change career, some had been called to move to other nations, some had rediscovered old, long-abandoned creative talents, and some had felt the stirrings to fight new battles in social justice. One lady had found her husband-to-be in the prayer room, and one had been given the name of her first son, over a year before he was born. Numerous lives reformatted, just from welcoming in the endlessly creative Spirit of God.

There were moments when the Shunammite woman must have regretted letting God reformat her existence, and I suspect many of my friends have had similar moments of doubt along the way. Our settled existence is comfortable, safe and predictable. It may not be brilliant in every aspect, but it works. As I am often heard to say, when rushing to finish something: 'It's not perfect but it'll do.'

Our God is a stickler for the best. He knows what is best for you, and he has your best interests at heart. He works in superlatives, longing to give you the richest, fullest life you can possibly take on board. That means two uncomfortable truths: first, you won't get everything you pray for, because some of what you pray for isn't the absolute best he can give you; second, from time to time he will thrust things into your hands which you aren't even sure you want. He isn't being cruel or pushy, and he will never force you to accept his reformatting. He is simply swapping out your 'it'll do' for his 'the best is yet to come'.

Praying it

Prayer can end up being almost as busy and productive a place as the rest of our lives sometimes. Prayer is, first and foremost, the place we go, within ourselves, to welcome the presence and power of God. That may involve talking, moving, singing or crying, but it must also involve stillness – waiting for him and letting him work.

Activity
Sometimes prayer just needs to be being. So the 'Action' for this section is inactivity. Find a comfortable, safe, distraction-free place to be, and rest in God's presence. Resist the temptation to 'do some praying'. Sit, lie or walk with him in companionable silence.

Talking it

- Has God ever given you something you hadn't prayed for and didn't want?
- Have you ever made a practical change in your life, to make more space for God's presence?
- Is it ever right to ask God to give someone something you know they don't want?

Living it

24-7 Prayer
Church life can get as busy as our personal lives can, and it is worth considering the possibility of programming in seasons for the whole church to stop and pray. Get together with a few others and plan a 24-7 Prayer week for your church. All you need is a room, some materials for creative prayer and a sign-up sheet. To find out more, visit www.24-7prayer.com.

Practising hospitality
Had the Shunammite woman not welcomed Elisha as her house-guest, perhaps she wouldn't have received some of the blessings she

did receive. One way to welcome God's presence is to welcome God's people. Make time and space this week to invite people to your home for a meal or a coffee.

The pursuit of resurrection
2 Kings 4:18–37

> **These, though commended by God for their great faith, did not receive what was promised. That promise has awaited us, who receive the better thing that God has provided in *these last days*, so that with us, our forebears might finally see the promise completed.**
> HEBREWS 11:39–40 (THE VOICE)

When I started working for The Salvation Army, I met a lady who became a firm friend and mentor. Her name was Jo, and she had come to know Jesus during her teenage years. She threw herself into her new-found faith with gusto, and as soon as she and her husband got married, they went to the William Booth Training College to become Salvation Army officers. I will never forget her telling me of her disappointment when she first saw the college curriculum. You see, her discipleship thus far had been straightforward: you read the Bible, you see what Jesus did, and then you go out and do likewise. Where then, she wondered, as she perused her Cadet Timetable were the classes on how to raise the dead? If that's what Jesus did, why wouldn't a Christian ministers' training college be teaching her how to do that?

For Jo, resurrection wasn't something that you waited for like the Number 7 bus. It was something you pursued. When something God had given her looked like it might have died, her first assumption was not to let go of it, but to seek to see it raised from the dead, because she believed life was meant to outweigh death. I think she and the Shunammite woman would have got on rather well.

It wasn't a con-trick after all. Elisha's word had come true, and a new baby boy had arrived in the home of the couple from Shunem. Yet the 'happily ever after' was still a world away, and never more so than on the day when the servants carried the boy home to his mother, suffering from a severe headache, only for him to die in her arms. Did she rue the day God had toppled her from her comfortable 'it'll do' existence, only to leave her here, a grieving parent with a hole no amount of comfort could fill? We're told nothing of how she felt, only what she did, because this lady was an activist. What followed was a pursuit of resurrection. Instead of settling to her mourning, she allowed God's Spirit to propel her into action.

But first, she left her boy in Elisha's room – that place which had come to signify the presence of God's power. How often do we try to fix things first, then hand them over to God when we don't get anywhere? Prayer should be our first resort, not our last. When something looks like it has died, take it straight to him in prayer, because he alone can restore life.

When she closed that bedroom door, the Shunammite woman set out on a course of action from which she refused to be diverted or distracted. She wouldn't tell her husband what had happened or what she was planning, presumably because she thought he might try to talk her out of it. And she wouldn't tell Gehazi, Elisha's servant, what was wrong, because she knew Elisha was the one she needed to talk to; she had no intention of bothering with go-betweens.

Time after time, my mobile phone would ring from the depths of my handbag and it would be Jo telling me to 'mobilise the troops'. Something had happened, and resurrection or breakthrough of some kind was needed. She didn't stop to worry or mourn; she didn't get sidetracked. She just got on the phone and rallied as much prayer as she possibly could. For Jo, prayer was a force to be taken seriously, and it deserved all the effort and energy we could give it.

It would have been the done thing to go and plead the help of a man of God, if a relative fell ill or died, but when the Shunammite woman reached Elisha, there was no humble begging. She more or less told him off for getting her hopes up in the first place. Just because we're pursuing resurrection, doesn't mean we aren't allowed to feel anger about the death or sorrow at the loss. Those feelings are healthy and normal, and it is entirely possible to feel them while also pursuing the miracle of resurrection.

It's fascinating that the seer-prophet wasn't told why the woman was coming to him. Elisha was perhaps the most powerful prophet in all of the Old Testament – even able to discern what the king was saying in his bedroom – yet he wasn't given access to this woman's secrets. There's no explanation as to why, but I like to think it was God's gentle recompense for the way Elisha and Gehazi had pried into her business, right at the start of the story. This was her story, not theirs; this resurrection was hers to pursue.

Having done all she could, she let God have the final word. She didn't follow Elisha into the room and critique his technique. She trusted God to do what he wanted to do through his prophet.

One dreadful day in June 2009, my friend Jo developed the same kind of headache the Shunammite boy had died from. Their stories ended very differently. The Shunammite boy was raised from the dead, but Jo suffered two brain aneurysms and died a few weeks later. Knowing her passionate opinions on resurrection, we prayed. We prayed while she was alive and we prayed after she died, but for her, resurrection happened the heavenward side of death.

Despite that, she has left with me a deep conviction that I always want to be someone who pursues resurrection. I know it won't always happen. I know that death is a part of life, and that I need not fear it. I know that there will be times when I need to let things die, so that new things can be born. But I never want to be someone who forgets that my God can and does raise the dead.

In C.S. Lewis' *The Lion, The Witch and the Wardrobe*, Aslan explains to Susan and Lucy how he was able to defeat death, and why the witch didn't see it coming.

> Though the witch knew the deep magic, there is a magic deeper still which she did not know. Her knowledge goes back only to the dawn of time. But if she could have looked a little further back, into the stillness and the darkness before time dawned, she would have read there a different incantation. She would have known that when a willing victim who had committed no treachery was killed in a traitor's stead, the table would crack and death itself would start working backwards.

On a glorious day, almost 2,000 years ago, God's own son was raised from the dead. Because of that one timeless explosion of life, the very processes of death have begun to work backwards. Death no longer has the final word. Life is forever and always stronger than death, brighter than death, weightier than death. Death only exists to allow in even more life.

Faith is leaping off the end of ourselves and believing that impossible dreams can come true, but no amount of positive attitude or wishful thinking will ever keep us living that sort of faith. That faith is rooted in and fuelled by the resurrection of Jesus. If God could raise Christ from the dead, sluicing the poison of death right out of creation altogether, then absolutely anything truly is possible.

One of the things I am most looking forward to when I get my new body with eyes that work is driving through the streets of God's newly created city in a high-powered sports car. (It's my love of the adrenalin rush again!) But I think I will slow down to pick up the Shunammite woman and my friend Jo, when I spot them.

The three of us may have lived very different lives, but we have all been writing the same story. We have all chosen to pursue resurrection, refusing to believe that the brokenness of this world is the best there is. We have all made it our business to chase after that 'better thing' which the writer to the Hebrews talks about (Hebrews 11:40), because we have all been convinced that the best is yet to come. And when that best has come, when the promise has been completed and fulfilled, and pain and sorrow are no more, we will be there at the party to celebrate.

And if that's the kind of faith you want to live, there'll be a spare seat in the sports car for you, too!

Praying it

We return to fire for our final prayer activity. It symbolises the presence of God, but it is also a wonderful image of death and resurrection. It consumes, but as it does so it produces light, heat, colour and energy – all things we associate with life.

Activity
If possible, acquire a firework or some sparklers; if not, use a candle. As you ignite, think of the things in life which feel as though they're dying and commit them into God's hands. As the flames take hold, pray that God will bring resurrection and new life, even in the midst of death.

Talking it

- Have you ever had an experience of something you thought was dead being resurrected? Was it a good thing?
- If Jesus broke the power of death, why doesn't God always heal people or raise them from the dead here on earth?
- What are you most looking forward to about heaven?

Living it

Resurrection hope
Do you know someone who is facing the death of something or someone dear to them at the moment? What could you do to help bring hope and comfort at this time?

More hero stories
The Bible is full of heroes we haven't had space to meet in this book. Why not look up a few more, and get yourself into a habit of reading about one of them each week, exploring their story and gleaning some encouragements and challenges for your own life.

BRF

Transforming
lives and communities

Christian growth and understanding of the Bible

Resourcing individuals, groups and leaders in churches for their own spiritual journey and for their ministry

Church outreach in the local community

Offering three programmes that churches are embracing to great effect as they seek to engage with their local communities and transform lives

Teaching Christianity in primary schools

Working with children and teachers to explore Christianity creatively and confidently

Children's and family ministry

Working with churches and families to explore Christianity creatively and bring the Bible alive

Visit **brf.org.uk** for more information on BRF's work

brf.org.uk